The BEGINNER'S GUIDE TO MOSAIC KNITTING

I0877524

LEISURE ARTS, INC. • Maumelle, Arkansas

MEET
Melissa Leapman

With more than 800 knit and crochet designs in print, Melissa Leapman is one of the most widely published American designers working today.

She began her design career by freelancing for leading ready-to-wear design houses in New York City. She also created designs to help top yarn companies promote their new and existing yarns each season. Her ability to quickly develop fully envisioned garments put her skills in great demand.

Through the years, Leisure Arts has published more than 40 books of Melissa's fabulous designs. Melissa is also the host of several Leisure Arts DVDs in the best-selling teach-yourself series, *"I Can't Believe I'm Knitting"* and *"I Can't Believe I'm Crocheting."*

Nationally, her designs have been featured in numerous magazines, and her workshops on knitting and crochet are consistently popular with crafters of all skill levels. She has taught at major events such as STITCHES, Vogue Knitting LIVE, and The Knitting Guild Association conferences, as well as at hundreds of yarn shops and local guild events across the country.

Look for other Leisure Arts books featuring Melissa's designs at www.leisurearts.com/meet-the-designers/melissa-leapman.html.

Learn to create complex-looking fabrics using just one color per row!

The BEGINNER'S GUIDE TO MOSAIC KNITTING

BY MELISSA LEAPMAN

Mosaic knitting is a fun technique that uses simple slipped stitches to create beautiful, intricate-looking multicolor fabric. Slipping stitches elongates them, drawing them up lengthwise into subsequent rows and, when stripes are involved, gives the appearance of bringing a second color into a row of knitting that's worked with only one yarn. It's color knitting the easy way!

Mosaic Knitting Techniques

SLIPPING STITCHES

The convention in knitting is to always slip stitches **purlwise** unless told otherwise. Always insert your right-hand needle into the stitch that's about to be slipped as if you're about to purl it, that is, from **right** to **left** in the front of the stitch. This ensures that the stitch will be sitting on the needle in the proper orientation when it's time to work it later.

When working mosaic patterns, it is important to keep the working yarn to the **wrong** side of the fabric when slipping stitches.

On **right** side rows, keep the working yarn toward the **back**.

On **wrong** side rows, keep the working yarn toward the **front**.

As with other types of color knitting, mosaic knitting requires changing colors. For mosaic patterns, the colors change every two rows; in other words, the colorwork is based on two row stripes. What could be easier?

ATTACHING A NEW COLOR

Here's how to attach a new color:

To begin a stripe with a yarn color that isn't attached to your knitting yet, at the beginning of a knit row, drop the old color, insert your right-hand needle into the first stitch of the row as if you were about to knit, and leaving a 6" (15 cm) tail, grab the new yarn and simply use it to knit the first stitch.

For subsequent stripes using the same color, you will be able to carry the yarn from one stripe to the next without cutting it (and thereby reducing the number of yarn tails in the process).

To do: Carry the yarns **loosely** up the side of the fabric, bringing the new yarn up from **below**, letting the old one hang until you need it again two rows later.

TIP: *Usually, knitters pick up a new yarn from underneath the old one, but this technique can cause frustrating tangles. (Ask me how I know!) To eliminate some of the fuss, alternately pick up the new yarn from underneath the old one and the next time from above. You'll be untangling the yarns as you knit!*

MOSAIC CHARTS

While each of the patterns in this book are presented in text and chart form, many knitters prefer working from charts because they can easily visualize what the fabric is going to look like.

Here's how:

Each square of the charted grid corresponds to one stitch and each row of squares corresponds to one row of knitting.

Charts are read from the lower edge up, with the first row at the bottom of the chart and the last row at the top.

To keep track of where you are on the chart, use a common sticky note. Once a row is finished, simply move the sticky note up.

Right-side rows are read from **right-to-left**, and **wrong-side** rows are read from **left-to-right**.

Note: When working in the round rather than back and forth in rows, such as for the Hat on page 19, the **right** side of the fabric is always facing you, so all rounds of its chart are read from **right-to-left**.

Charts make it easy to see how many stitches are involved in a pattern. In some charts, bold boxes indicate the stitch repeat, and if extra stitches are required on each side to center the pattern, they are shown to the left and right of the repeat. In the Pullover, the Large Geometric Pattern on page 55 has a multiple of 8 plus 9 stitches; it is an 8-stitch repeat plus 9 extra stitches, one on the right-hand side and 8 on the left-hand side, which center the pattern properly.

Within each box of the chart is a symbol which indicates the way a stitch will be worked. In Mosaic Knitting, stitches will be knitted, purled, or slipped. For the charts in this book, you'll only need to be familiar with three symbols!

All rows in charts are shown as they appear on the **public** side of the fabric. Therefore, the same symbol means different things on right-side and wrong-side rows. The blank box, for instance, represents a knit stitch on a right-side row, but if you're on a wrong-side row and want the stitch to appear as a knit stitch on the reverse side of the fabric, you must purl it. If a symbol is used on both right- and wrong-side rows of the chart, the stitch key will tell you which knitting maneuver to use where. There's no need to memorize anything!

For ease of use, different colored squares indicated different colors of yarn.

TEXTURES

Mosaic knitting is amazingly versatile. Knitters have the choice of three different fabric textures: stockinette-based, garter-based, or a cool combination of the two in which the background color is smooth stockinette and the garter patternwork sits on top of the fabric. Best of all, any mosaic pattern can be worked in any of the three different textures! The only difference is how the wrong-side rows are worked.

SMOOTH, STOCKINETTE-BASED FABRIC

The simplest mosaic patterns use a stockinette stitch base for the fabric: On **right-side** rows, stitches are either knitted or slipped with the yarn in **back** of the fabric; on **wrong-side** rows, stitches are purled or slipped with the yarn **towards** you, on the purl side of the fabric. The result is that all stitches—those in the background as well as the contrasting patterned ones—are smooth like stockinette, and all yarn "floats" sit on the wrong-side.

Notice how the working yarn is always where it needs to be when slipping stitches; there's no need to move it since it is already toward the **wrong-side** of the fabric, even on wrong side rows.

Here's a sample chart *(CHART A)* showing a stockinette-based mosaic pattern.

CHART A: STOCKINETTE-BASED MOSAIC

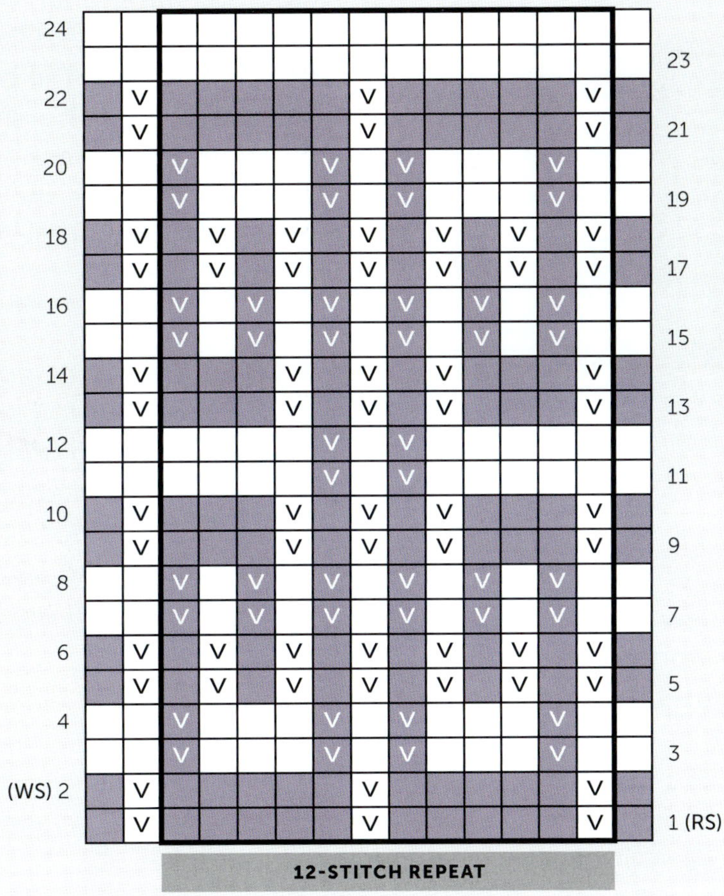

COLOR KEY

■ = A

□ = B

STITCH KEY

□ = Knit on RS; purl on WS

V = Slip st purlwise WYB on RS rows; slip st purlwise WYF on WS rows

BUMPY, GARTER-BASED FABRIC

In this type of mosaic knitting, all stitches on every row are either knitted or slipped; they are **never** purled. This creates a textured, non-curling fabric that resembles garter stitch.

It's important to remember that the working yarn must **always** be on the **wrong-side** of the fabric when slipping the stitches: On **right-side** rows, the yarn remains in the **back** of the work at all times, but on **wrong-side** rows, the yarn must be brought **towards** the knitter, on the **wrong-side** of the fabric, as stitches are slipped. Remember, the goal is to never make floats on the public side of the fabric!

Here's the same chart *(CHART B)* shown earlier revised for a garter-based fabric. Notice that the only difference is the dots on **wrong-side** rows. These indicate that the stitches will be knitted, so be sure to move the working yarn before and after slipping stitches on the wrong-side rows!

NOTE: *When moving the working yarn from front to back and vice versa, be sure to bring it between the tips of the needles and not over the right-hand needle! Otherwise, you'll be creating a yarn over which will make a great big hole in your work.*

CHART B: **GARTER-BASED MOSAIC**

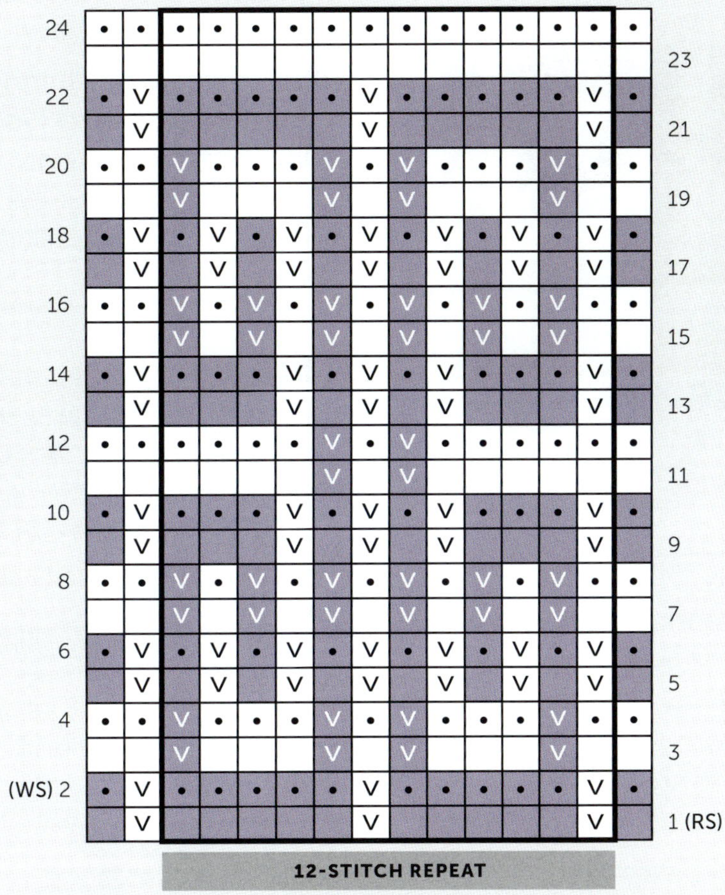

COLOR KEY

- [shaded] = A
- [blank] = B

STITCH KEY

- [blank] = Knit on RS
- • = Knit on WS
- V = Slip st purlwise WYB on RS rows; slip st purlwise WYF on WS rows

COMBINATION STOCKINETTE AND GARTER FABRIC

To create highly-textured patterns, work the background color in stockinette stitch and the contrast color in garter stitch.

In these beautiful fabrics, **right-side** rows are worked the same way as for other mosaic patterns, always slipping stitches with the working yarn towards the **back** of the fabric; on **wrong-side** rows, background-colored stitches are purled but the contrast-colored stitches are knitted. On those contrast-colored rows, be sure to bring the working yarn **towards** the **front** of the work. Remember, the goal is to keep all yarn floats toward the **wrong** side of the fabric.

Here's that same chart *(CHART C)* revised for this third type of textured fabric. Notice that only the wrong-side rows are changed. One color is knitted on the wrong-side rows, and the other one is purled.

> **TIP:** *When first learning how to read knitting charts, it can be useful to keep the text version of the pattern handy. This way you can compare the two versions!*

PROJECTS

Knit the following 8 projects as you discover how easy and fun mosaic knitting can be!

CHART C: COMBINATION MOSAIC

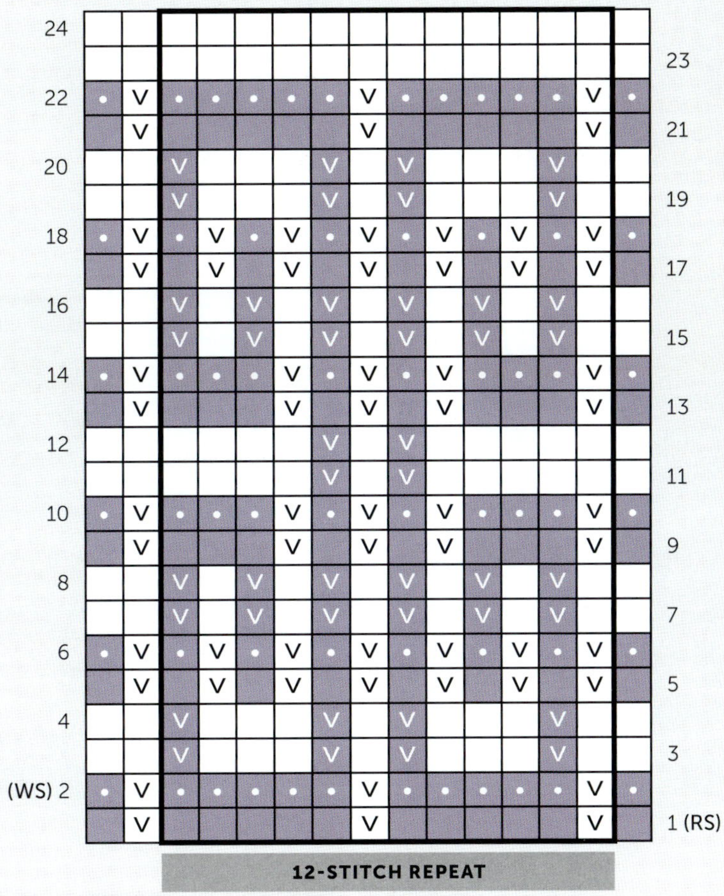

COLOR KEY

- ▒ = A
- ☐ = B

STITCH KEY

- ☐ = Knit on RS; purl on WS
- • = Knit on WS
- V = Slip st purlwise WYB on RS rows; slip st purlwise WYF on WS rows

Contents

3 | Meet the Designer

5 | The Beginner's Guide to Mosaic Knitting

22

Cowl

28

Wrap

40

Sampler Throw

52

Pullover

16

Headband

18

Hat

32

Cresent Shawl

36

Baby Blanket

58 | General Instructions

64 | Yarn Information

HEADBAND

(garter-based fabric)

EASY

Finished Measurement:
3½" wide x 20" circumference (9 cm x 51 cm)

Gauge Information:
In Linked Chains Pattern, 17 sts = 3½" (9 cm)

SHOPPING LIST

- **Yarn** (Medium Weight) 4 MEDIUM **[**5 ounces, 251 yards (142 grams, 230 meters) per skein**]**:
  - Color A (Green)-1 skein
  - Color B (Purple)-1 skein
- **Knitting Needles**
  - Size 8 (5 mm) **or** size needed for gauge
- **Additional Supplies**
  - Yarn needle

NOTES:

Always slip stitches **purlwise** (page 6) with the yarn to the **wrong** side of the fabric.

On **wrong** side rows, be sure to move the working yarn to the **front** before slipping stitches and then to the **back** to resume knitting.

When changing color, do **not** cut the yarn; instead, carry the yarn loosely up the side of the fabric.

HEADBAND

With Color B, cast on 17 sts.

Row 1 (Right side)**:** With Color A, K4, ★ slip 1 as if to **purl** WYB, K1, slip 1 as if to **purl**, K3; repeat from ★ across to last st, K1.

Row 2: With Color A, K1, ★ K3, slip 1 as if to **purl** WYF, K1, slip 1 as if to **purl**; repeat from ★ across to last 4 sts, K4.

Row 3: With Color B, (K1, slip 1 as if to **purl** WYB) twice, ★ K3, slip 1 as if to **purl** WYB, K1, slip 1 as if to **purl** WYB; repeat from ★ across to last st, K1.

Row 4: With Color B, K1, ★ slip 1 as if to **purl** WYF, K1, slip 1 as if to **purl** WYF, K3; repeat from ★ across to last 4 sts, (slip 1 as if to **purl** WYF, K1) twice.

Row 5: With Color A, K2, slip 1 as if to **purl** WYB, K1, ★ K4, slip 1 as if to **purl** WYB, K1; repeat from ★ across to last st, K1.

Row 6: With Color A, K1, ★ K1, slip 1 as if to **purl** WYF, K4; repeat from ★ across to last 4 sts, K1, slip 1 as if to **purl** WYF, K2.

Row 7: With Color B, K4, ★ K1, slip 1 as if to **purl** WYB, K4; repeat from the ★ across to last st, K1.

Row 8: With Color B, K1, ★ K4, slip 1 as if to **purl** WYF, K1; repeat from ★ across to last 4 sts, K4.

Rows 9 and 10: Repeat Rows 5 and 6.

Rows 11 and 12: Repeat Rows 3 and 4.

Rows 13-16: Repeat Rows 1-4.

Repeat Rows 1-16 for pattern until piece measures approximately 20" (51 cm) from cast on edge, ending by working a **wrong** side row.

Bind off all sts in **knit**, leaving a long end for sewing.

With **right** side facing, sew the cast on edge to the bind off edge.

Linked Chains Pattern
(see CHART D below)
(multiple of 6 + 5 sts)

Use the text above or refer to the chart below.

CHART D: LINKED CHAINS

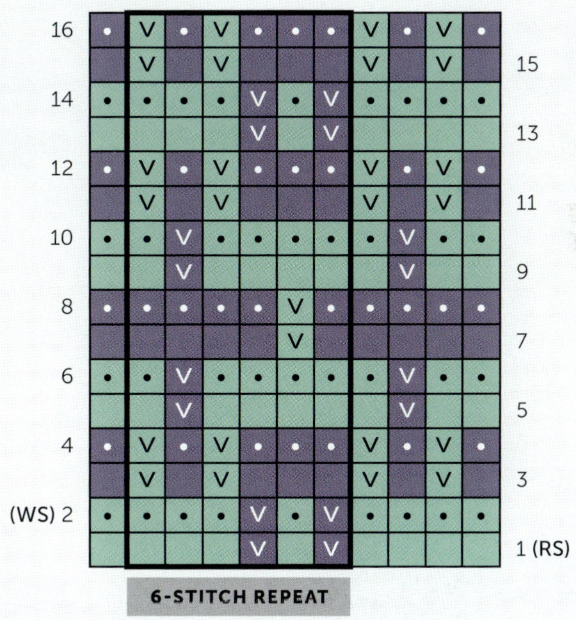

COLOR KEY

- (green) = A
- (purple) = B

STITCH KEY

- (blank) = Knit on RS
- • = Knit on WS
- V = Slip st purlwise WYB on RS rows; slip st purlwise WYF on WS rows

HAT

(stockinette-based fabric)

EASY

Finished Measurement:
One size fits most women

Gauge Information:
With larger size needle, in Greek Key Pattern, 22 sts = 3½" (9 cm)

Technique Used:
K2 tog ***(Fig. 3, page 61)***

SHOPPING LIST

- **Yarn** (Medium Weight) 4 MEDIUM **[**3 ounces, 197 yards (85 grams, 180 meters) per skein**]**:
  - Color A (Red)-1 skein
  - Color B (Off White)-1 skein
- **Knitting Needles**
  16" (40.5 cm) Circular,
  - Size 6 (4 mm) **and**
  - Size 8 (5 mm) **or** size needed for gauge

  Double-Pointed (set of 5),
  - Size 8 (5 mm) **or** size needed for gauge
- **Additional Supplies**
  - Faux Fur pom pom
  - Yarn needle

HAT

RIBBING

With smaller size circular needle and Color B, cast on 96 sts; place a marker to indicate the beginning of the round ***(see Markers and Using Circular Needles, page 60)***.

Rnd 1 (Right side)**:** (K2, P2) around.

Repeat Rnd 1 for K2, P2 Rib Pattern, until Ribbing measures approximately 1¼" (3 cm) from cast on edge.

NOTES:

The Hat is made in the round from the bottom up.

Always slip stitches **purlwise** (page 6) with the yarn to the **wrong** side of the fabric.

When changing color, do **not** cut the yarn; instead, carry the yarn loosely up the wrong side of the fabric.

When decreasing for the crown, change to double-pointed needles when there are too few stitches remaining to knit comfortably with the circular needle.

BODY

Change to larger size circular needle.

Rnds 1 and 2: With Color A, knit around.

Rnds 3 and 4: With Color B, ★ K5, slip 1 as if to **purl**; repeat from ★ around.

Rnds 5 and 6: With Color A, ★ slip 1 as if to **purl**, K3, slip 1 as if to **purl**, K1; repeat from ★ around.

Rnds 7 and 8: With Color B, ★ K1, slip 1 as if to **purl**, K3, slip 1 as if to **purl**; repeat from ★ around.

Rnds 9 and 10: With Color A, ★ slip 1 as if to **purl**, K5; repeat from ★ around.

Rnds 11 and 12: With Color B, knit around.

Repeat Rnds 1-12 for Greek Key Pattern until piece measures approximately 9½" (24 cm) from cast on edge, by working Rnd 10 **or** Rnd 12.

CROWN

Rnd 1: With Color B, (K 10, K2 tog) around: 88 sts.

Rnd 2: (K9, K2 tog) around: 80 sts.

Rnd 3: (K8, K2 tog) around: 72 sts.

Rnd 4: (K7, K2 tog) around: 64 sts.

Rnd 5: (K6, K2 tog) around: 56 sts.

Rnd 6: (K5, K2 tog) around: 48 sts.

Rnd 7: (K4, K2 tog) around: 40 sts.

Rnd 8: (K3, K2 tog) around: 32 sts.

Rnd 9: (K2, K2 tog) around: 24 sts.

Rnd 10: (K1, K2 tog) around: 16 sts.

Rnd 11: K2 tog around: 8 sts.

Cut yarn, leaving a long end for sewing.

Thread yarn needle with long end and weave end through remaining sts; gather **tightly** and secure end.

Greek Key Pattern
(see CHART E below)
(worked in the round on a multiple of 6 sts)

Use the Body text above or refer to the chart below.

CHART E: GREEK KEY

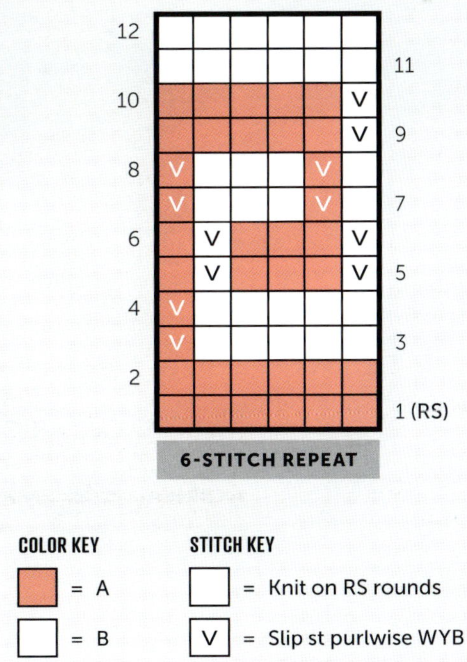

COWL

(one with garter-based fabric & one with stockinette-based fabric)

EASY

Finished Measurement:
One size fits most women

Gauge Information:
With larger size needle, in Little Boxes Pattern, 18 sts = 4" (10 cm)

SHOPPING LIST

- **Yarn** (Medium Weight) 4 MEDIUM
  [5 ounces, 251 yards (142 grams, 230 meters) per skein**]**:
  - Color A (Aqua)-1 skein
  - Color B (Pink)-1 skein
  - Color C (Mint)-1 skein
  - Color D (Tan)-1 skein
- **Knitting Needles**
  16" (40.5 cm) Circular,
  - Size 6 (4 mm) **and**
  - Size 8 (5 mm) **or** sizes needed for gauge
- **Additional Supplies**
  - Yarn needle

NOTES:

The cowl is made in the round from the bottom up.

Always slip stitches **purlwise** (page 6) with the yarn to the **wrong** side of the fabric.

When changing color, do **not** cut the yarn; instead, carry the yarn loosely up the **wrong** side of the fabric.

GARTER COWL

BORDER

Using smaller circular needle and Color A, cast on 100 sts; place a marker to indicate the beginning of the round ***(see Markers and Using Circular Needles, page 60)***.

Rnd 1 (Right side)**:** Knit around.

Rnd 2: Purl around.

Rnds 3 and 4: Repeat Rnds 1 and 2.

BODY

Change to larger circular needle.

Rnd 1 (Right side)**:** With Color B, knit around.

Rnd 2: With Color B, purl around.

Rnd 3: With Color C, ★ slip 1 as if to **purl** WYB, K3; repeat from ★ around.

Rnd 4: With Color C, ★ slip 1 as if to **purl** WYB, P3; repeat from ★ around.

Rnd 5: With Color B, ★ K1, slip 1 as if to **purl** WYB; repeat from ★ around.

Rnd 6: With Color B, ★ P1, slip 1 as if to **purl** WYB; repeat from ★ around.

Rnd 7: With Color C, ★ slip 1 as if to **purl** WYB, K3; repeat from ★ around.

Rnd 8: With Color C, ★ slip 1 as if to **purl** WYB, P3; repeat from ★ around.

Rnd 9: With Color B, knit around.

Rnd 10: With Color B, purl around.

Rnd 11: With Color A, knit around.

Rnd 12: With Color A, purl around.

Rnd 13: With Color D, ★ slip 1 as if to **purl** WYB, K3; repeat from ★ around.

Rnd 14: With Color D, ★ slip 1 as if to **purl** WYB, P3; repeat from ★ around.

Rnd 15: With Color A, ★ K1, slip one as if to **purl** WYB; repeat from ★ around.

Rnd 16: With Color A, ★ P1, slip 1 as if to **purl** WYB; repeat from ★ around.

Rnd 17: With Color D, ★ slip 1 as if to **purl** WYB, K3; repeat from ★ around.

Rnd 18: With Color D, ★ slip 1 as if to **purl** WYB, P3; repeat from ★ around.

Rnd 19: With Color A, knit around.

Rnd 20: With Color A, purl around.

Repeat Rnds 1-20 for the pattern until piece measures approximately 8½" (21.5 cm) from cast on edge, ending by working Rnd 10 **or** Rnd 20.

CHART F: LITTLE BOXES (garter)

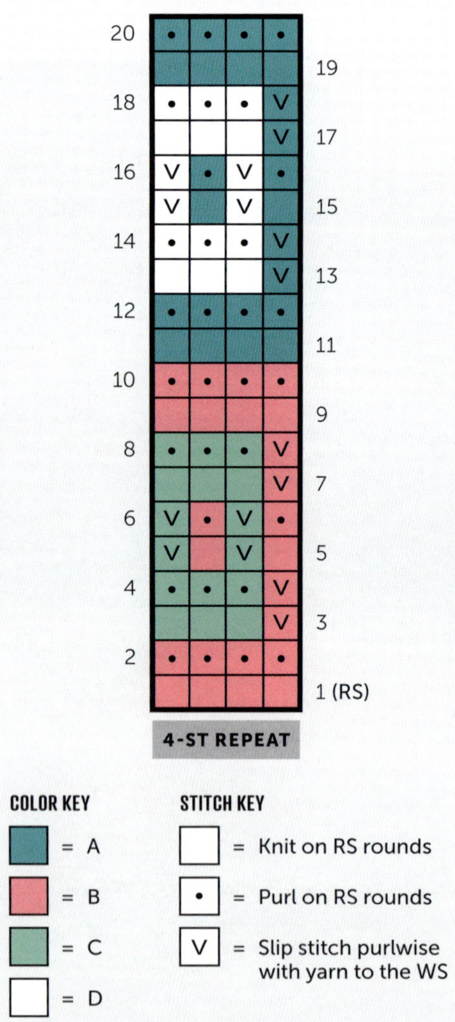

BORDER

Change to smaller circular needle.

Rnd 1: With Color B, knit around.

Rnd 2: Purl around.

Rnds 3 and 4: Repeat Rnds 1 and 2.

Bind off all sts in **knit**.

Little Boxes Pattern
(see CHART F on page 24)
(worked in the round on a multiple of 4 sts)

Use the Body text, page 23, or refer to the chart, page 24.

STOCKINETTE COWL

BORDER

With Color A, work same as Garter-Based Cowl, page 22.

BODY

Change to larger circular needle.

Rnds 1 and 2: With Color B, knit around.

Rnds 3 and 4: With Color C, ★ slip 1 as if to **purl** WYB, K3; repeat from ★ around.

Rnds 5 and 6: With Color B, ★ K1, slip 1 as if to **purl** WYB; repeat from ★ around.

Rnd 6: With Color B, ★ P1, slip 1 as if to **purl** WYB; repeat from ★ around.

Rnds 7 and 8: With Color C, ★ slip 1 as if to **purl** WYB, K3; repeat from ★ around.

Rnds 9 and 10: With Color B, knit around.

Rnds 11 and 12: With Color A, knit around.

Rnds 13 and 14: With Color D, ★ slip 1 as if to **purl** WYB, K3; repeat from ★ around.

Rnds 15 and 16: With Color A, ★ K1, slip one as if to **purl** WYB; repeat from ★ around.

CHART G: LITTLE BOXES (stockinette)

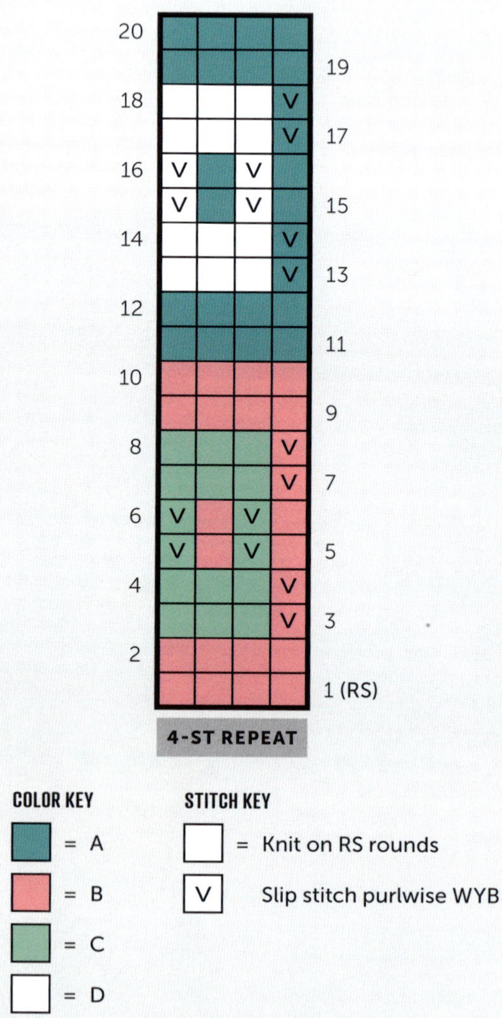

Rnds 17 and 18: With Color D, ★ slip 1 as if to **purl** WYB, K3; repeat from ★ around.

Rnds 19 and 20: With Color A, knit around.

Repeat Rnds 1-20 for the pattern until piece measures approximately 8½" (21.5 cm) from cast on edge, ending by working Rnd 10 **or** Rnd 20.

BORDER

Change to smaller circular needle.

Rnd 1: With Color B, knit around.

Rnd 2: Purl around.

Rnds 3 and 4: Repeat Rnds 1 and 2.

Bind off all sts in **knit**.

Little Boxes Pattern
(see CHART G at left)
(worked in the round on a multiple of 4 sts)

See chart at left or follow the Body text, page 26.

WRAP

(combination stockinette and garter-based fabric)

EASY

Finished Measurement:
24" x 68" (61 cm x 173 cm)

Gauge Information:
With larger size needle, in Small Geometric Pattern, 16 sts = 4" (10 cm) wide

Technique Used:
M1 ***(Figs. 6a & b, page 62)***

SHOPPING LIST

- **Yarn** (Medium Weight) 4 MEDIUM **[**3.5 ounces, 170 yards (100 grams, 156 meters) per skein**]**:
  - Color A (Red)-2 skeins
  - Color B (Gold)-2 skeins
  - Color C (Mint)-5 skeins
  - Color D (Off White)-2 skeins
- **Knitting Needles**
  16" (40.5 cm) **and** 36" (91.5 cm) Circular,
  - Size 8 (5 mm) **and**
  - Size 9 (5.5 mm) **or** sizes needed for gauge
- **Additional Supplies**
  - Yarn needle

WRAP

BODY

With larger size needle and Color A, cast on 79 sts.

Rows 1 and 2: With Color A, knit across.

Row 3 (Right side)**:** With Color B, knit across.

Row 4: With Color B, purl across.

Row 5: With Color A, K1, ★ slip 1 as if to **purl** WYB, K3; repeat from ★ across to last 2 sts, slip 1 as if to **purl** WYB, K1.

Row 6: With Color A, K1, slip 1 as if to **purl** WYF, ★ K3, slip 1 as if to **purl** WYF; repeat from ★ across to last st, K1.

Row 7: With Color B, K1, ★ K1, slip 1 as if to **purl** WYB; repeat from ★ across to last 2 sts, K2.

NOTES:

Always slip stitches **purlwise** (page 6) with the yarn to the **wrong** side of the fabric.

When changing color, do **not** cut the yarn; instead, carry the yarn loosely up the side of the fabric.

The circular needle is used to accommodate the large number of stitches. Do **not** join at the end of the rows; instead, work back and forth in rows.

Row 8: With Color B, P2, ★ slip 1 as if to **purl** WYF, P1; repeat from ★ across to last st, P1.

Row 9: With Color A, K1, ★ K2, slip 1 as if to **purl** WYB, K1; repeat from ★ across to last 2 sts, K2.

Row 10: With Color A, K2, ★ K1, slip 1 as if to **purl** WYF, K2; repeat from ★ across to last st, K1.

Rows 11 and 12: Repeat Rows 3 and 4.

Rows 13 and 14: With Color A, knit across.

Rows 15 and 16: With Color C, knit across.

Row 17: With Color D, knit across.

Row 18: With Color D, purl across.

Row 19: With Color C, K1, ★ slip 1 as if to **purl** WYB, K3; repeat from ★ across to last 2 sts, slip 1 as if to **purl** WYB, K1.

Row 20: With Color C, K1, slip 1 as if to **purl** WYF, ★ K3, slip 1 as if to **purl** WYF; repeat from ★ across to last st, K1.

Row 21: With Color D, K1, ★ K1, slip 1 as if to **purl** WYB; repeat from ★ across to last 2 sts, K2.

Row 22: With Color D, P2, ★ slip 1 as if to **purl** WYF, P1; repeat from ★ across to last st, P1.

Row 23: With Color C, K1, ★ K2, slip 1 as if to **purl** WYB, K1; repeat from ★ across to last 2 sts, K2.

Row 24: With Color C, K2, ★ K1, slip 1 as if to **purl** WYF, K2; repeat from ★ across to last st, K1.

Rows 25 and 26: Repeat Rows 3 and 4.

Rows 27 and 28: With Color C, knit across.

Repeat Rows 1-28 for the pattern until piece measures approximately 64" (162.5 cm) from cast on edge, ending by working Row 14.

Bind off all sts in **knit**.

EDGING

SHORT SIDE

With **right** facing, using smaller size needle and Color C, pick up 72 sts (or an even number of sts) evenly spaced across one short side of the Body ***(Figs. 7a & b, page 63)***.

Row 1 (Wrong side)**:** Knit across.

Row 2 (Increase row)**:** K1, M1, knit across to last st, M1, K1: 74 sts.

Rows 3-20: Repeat Rows 1 and 2, 9 times: 92 sts.

Bind off all sts in **knit**.

Repeat across opposite short side.

LONG SIDE

With **right** facing and smaller size needle, pick up 232 sts (or an even number of sts) along one long side of the Body.

Work same as for Short Side: 252 sts.

Repeat across other long side.

Sew each mitered corner.

Small Geometric Pattern

(see CHART H below)

(multiple of 4 + 3 stitches)

Use the Body text, page 29, or follow the chart below.

CHART H: SMALL GEOMETRIC

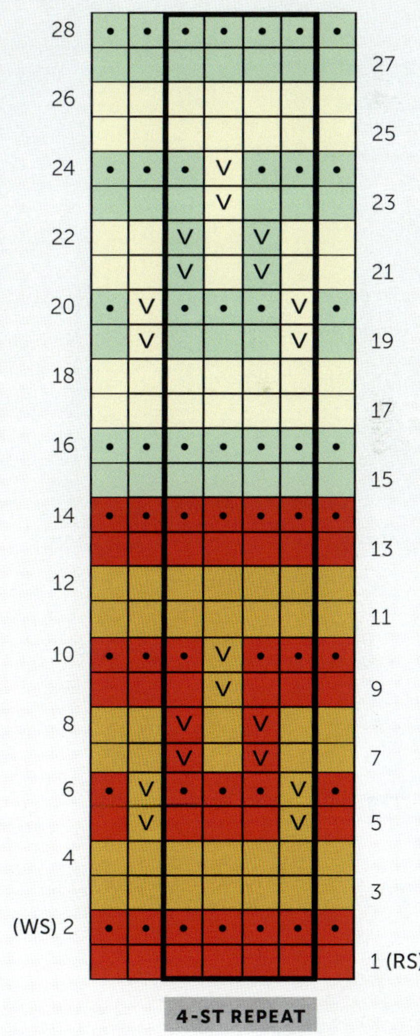

COLOR KEY

- = A
- = B
- = C
- = D

STITCH KEY

- ☐ = Knit on RS; purl on WS
- • = Purl on RS; knit on WS
- V = Slip stitch purlwise with yarn to the WS

CRESENT SHAWL

(garter-based fabric)

EASY

Finished Measurement:
84" (213.5 cm) wide

Gauge Information:
In the Turkish Tiles Pattern,
23 sts = 4" (10 cm)

Techniques Used:
K2 tog ***(Fig. 3, page 61)***
P2 tog ***(Fig. 4, page 61)***
SSK ***(Figs. 5a-c, page 62)***

SHOPPING LIST

- **Yarn** (Light Weight) [3.5 ounces, 254 yards (100 grams, 232 meters) per skein]:
  - Color A (Gold)-1 skein
  - Color B (Fuchsia)-2 skeins
- **Knitting Needles**
  36" (91.5 cm) Circular,
  - Size 6 (4 mm) **or** size needed for gauge

SHAWL

BORDER

With Color A, cast on 483 sts.

Rows 1-4: Knit across.

Body

Row 1(Right side)**:** With Color B, K1, ★ slip 1 as if to **purl** WYB, K9; repeat from ★ across to last 2 sts, slip 1 as if to **purl** WYB, K1.

Row 2: With Color B, K1, slip 1 as if to **purl** WYF, ★ K9, slip 1 as if to **purl** WYF; repeat from ★ across to last st, K1.

NOTES:

Always slip stitches **purlwise** (page 6) with the yarn to the **wrong** side of the fabric.

On **wrong** side rows, be sure to move the working yarn to the **front** before slipping stitches and then to the **back** to resume knitting.

When changing color, do **not** cut the yarn; instead, carry the yarn loosely up the side of the fabric.

The circular needle is used to accommodate the large number of stitches. Do not join at the end of the rows; instead, work back and forth in rows.

When working the short rows, always work until one stitch before the turning point of the previous row.

Row 3: With Color A, K1, ★ K1, slip 1 as if to **purl** WYB, K1, slip 1 as if to **purl** WYB, K3, slip 1 as if to **purl** WYB, K1, slip 1 as if to **purl** WYB; repeat from ★ across to last 2 sts, K2.

Row 4: With Color A, K2, ★ slip 1 as if to **purl** WYF, K1, slip 1 as if to **purl** WYF, K3, (slip 1 as if to **purl** WYF, K1) twice; repeat from ★ across to last st, K1.

Row 5: With Color B, K1, ★ slip 1 as if to **purl** WYB, K3, slip 1 as if to **purl** WYB, K1, slip 1 as if to **purl** WYB, K3; repeat from ★ across to last 2 sts, slip 1 as if to **purl** WYB, K1.

Row 6: With Color B, K1, slip 1 as if to **purl** WYF, ★ K3, slip 1 as if to **purl** WYF, K1, slip 1 as if to **purl** WYF, K3, slip 1 as if to **purl** WYF; repeat from ★ across last st, K1.

Row 7: With Color A, K1, ★ K1, slip 1 as if to **purl** WYB, (K3, slip 1 as if to **purl** WYB) twice; repeat from ★ across to last 2 sts, K2.

Row 8: With Color A, K2, ★ slip 1 as if to **purl** WYF, (K3, slip 1 as if to **purl** WYF) twice, K1; repeat from ★ across to last st, K1.

Row 9: With Color B, K1, ★ slip 1 as if to **purl** WYB, K1, slip 1 as if to **purl** WYB, K5, slip 1 as if to **purl** WYB, K1; repeat from ★ across to last 2 sts, slip 1 as if to **purl** WYB, K1.

Row 10: With Color B, K1, slip 1 as if to **purl** WYF, ★ K1, slip 1 as if to **purl** WYF, K5, slip 1 as if to **purl** WYF, K1, slip 1 as if to **purl** WYF; repeat from ★ across to last st, K1.

Row 11: With Color A, K1, ★ K1, slip 1 as if to **purl** WYB, (K3, slip 1 as if to **purl** WYB) twice; repeat from ★ across to last 2 sts, K2.

Row 12: With Color A, K2, ★ slip 1 as if to **purl** WYF, (K3, slip 1 as if to **purl** WYF) twice, K1; repeat from ★ across to last st, K1.

Row 13: With Color B, K1, ★ slip 1 as if to **purl** WYB, K3, slip 1 as if to **purl** WYB, K1, slip 1 as if to **purl** WYB, K3; repeat from ★ across last 2 sts, slip 1 as if to **purl** WYB, K1.

Row 14: With Color A, K1, slip 1 as if to **purl** WYF, ★ K3, slip 1 as if to **purl** WYF, K1, slip 1 as if to **purl** WYF, K3, slip 1 as if to **purl** WYF; repeat from ★ across to last st, K1.

Row 15: With Color A, K1, ★ K1, slip 1 as if to **purl** WYB, K1, slip 1 as if to **purl** WYB, K3, slip 1 as if to **purl** WYB, K1, slip 1 as if to **purl** WYB; repeat from ★ across to last 2 sts, K2.

Row 16: With Color A, K2, ★ slip 1 as if to **purl** WYF, K1, slip 1 as if to **purl** WYF, K3, (slip 1 as if to **purl** WYF, K1) twice; repeat from ★ across to last st, K1.

Row 17: With Color B, K1, ★ slip 1 as if to **purl** WYB, K9; repeat from ★ across to last 2 sts, slip 1 as if to **purl** WYB, K1.

Row 18: With Color B, K1, slip 1 as if to **purl** WYF, ★ K9, slip 1 as if to **purl** WYF; repeat from ★ across to last st, K1.

Rows 19 and 20: With Color A, knit across.

Row 21 (Decrease row)**:** With Color A, knit across decreasing 50 sts evenly spaced: 433 sts.

Row 22: With Color A, knit across.

Rows 23 and 24: Repeat Rows 21 and 22: 383 sts.

Cut Color A.

SHORT ROWS

Row 1 (Right side)**:** With Color B, K 196, turn.

Row 2: P 13, turn.

Row 3: K 12, SSK, K3, turn.

Row 4: P 15, P2 tog, P3, turn.

Row 5: K 18, SSK, K3, turn.

Row 6: P 21, P2 tog, P3, turn.

Row 7: Knit across to one stitch **before** the gap of the last turning point, SSK, K3, turn.

Row 8: Purl across to one stitch **before** the gap of the last turning point, P2 tog, P3, turn.

Repeat Rows 7 and 8, working 3 more stitches every row, until no stitches remain unworked at each edge.

Next Row (Right side)**:** K2 tog, knit across.

Last Row: Bind off as follows: ★ P2 tog, slip the stitch from the right-hand needle back onto the left-hand needle; repeat from ★ across.

Turkish Tiles Pattern
(see CHART I at right)
(multiple of 10 + 3 stitches)

Use the Border text, page 33, or refer to the chart at right.

CHART I: TURKISH TILES

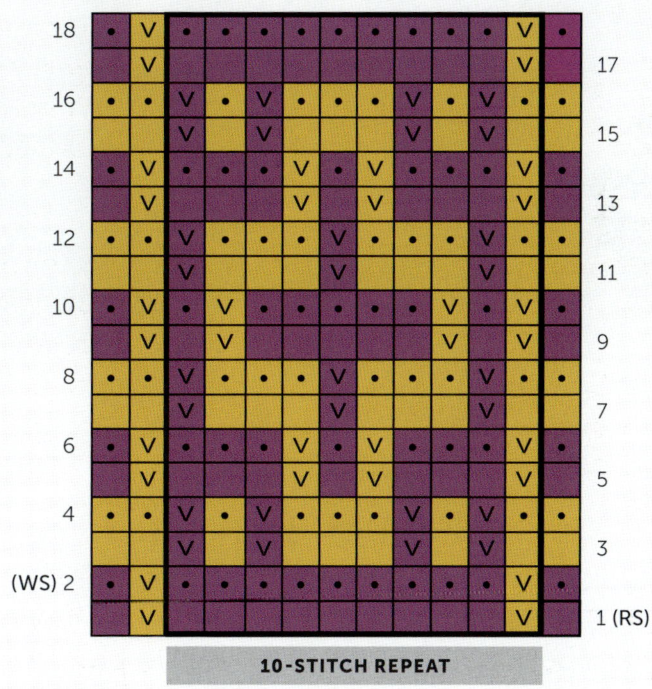

COLOR KEY

= A

= B

STITCH KEY

= Knit on RS

• = Knit on WS

V = Slip stitch purlwise with yarn to the WS

BABY BLANKET

(stockinette-based fabric)

EASY

Finished Measurement:
36" wide x 42" long
(91.5 cm x 106.5 cm)

Gauge Information:
With larger size needle, in Jazzy Squares pattern, 18 sts = 4¼" (10.75 cm) wide

Technique Used:
M1 ***(Figs. 6a & b, page 62)***

SHOPPING LIST

- **Yarn** (Medium Weight) 4 MEDIUM **[**3.5 ounces, 170 yards (100 grams, 156 meters) per skein**]**:
  - Color A (Pink)-3 skeins
  - Color B (Grey)-4 skeins
- **Knitting Needles**
  36" (91.5 cm) Circular,
  - Size 8 (5 mm) **and**
  - Size 9 (5.5 mm) **or** sizes needed for gauge
- **Additional Supplies**
  - Yarn needle

BLANKET

BODY

With larger size needle and Color A, cast on 137 sts.

Row 1 (Right side)**:** With Color A, knit across.

Row 2: With Color A, purl across.

Row 3: With Color B, K1, ★ slip 1 as if to **purl** WYB, (K1, slip 1 as if to **purl** WYB) 4 times, K9; repeat from ★ across to last 10 sts, (slip 1 as if to **purl** WYB, K1) 5 times.

Row 4: With Color B, (P1, slip 1 as if to **purl** WYF) 5 times, ★ P9, slip 1 as if to **purl** WYF, (P1, slip 1 as if to **purl** WYF) 4 times; repeat from ★ across to last st, P1.

Rows 5-12: Repeat Rows 1-4 twice.

Row 13: With Color A, knit across.

NOTES:

Always slip stitches **purlwise** (page 6) with the yarn to the **wrong** side of the fabric.

When changing color, do **not** cut the yarn; instead, carry the yarn loosely up the side of the fabric.

The circular needle is used to accommodate the large number of stitches. Do **not** join at the end of the rows; instead, work back and forth in rows.

Row 14: With Color A, purl across.

Row 15: With Color B, K1, ★ K9, slip 1 as if to **purl** WYB, (K1, slip 1 as if to **purl** WYB) 4 times; repeat from ★ across to last 10 sts, K 10.

Row 16: With Color B, P 10, ★ slip 1 as if to **purl** WYF, (P1, slip 1 as if to **purl** WYF) 4 times, P9; repeat from ★ across to last st, P1.

Rows 17-24: Repeat Rows 13-16 twice.

Repeat Rows 1-24 for Jazzy Square Pattern until Body measures approximately 38" (96.5 cm) from cast on edge, ending by working Row 12 or Row 24.

Bind off all sts in **knit**.

EDGING

SHORT SIDE

With **right** facing, using smaller size needle and Color B, pick up 118 sts evenly spaced across one short side of the Body ***(Figs. 7a & b, page 63)***.

Row 1 (Wrong side)**:** Knit across.

Row 2 (Increase row)**:** K1, M1, knit across to last st, M1, K1: 120 sts.

Rows 3-20: Repeat Rows 1 and 2, 9 times: 138 sts.

Bind off all sts in **knit**.

Repeat across opposite short side.

LONG SIDE

With **right** facing and smaller size needle, pick up 138 sts along one long side of the Body.

Work same as for Short Side: 158 sts.

Repeat across other long side.

Sew each mitered corner.

Jazzy Squares Pattern
(see CHART J below)
(multiple of 18 + 11 sts)

Use the Body text, page 37, or follow the chart below.

CHART J: JAZZY SQUARES

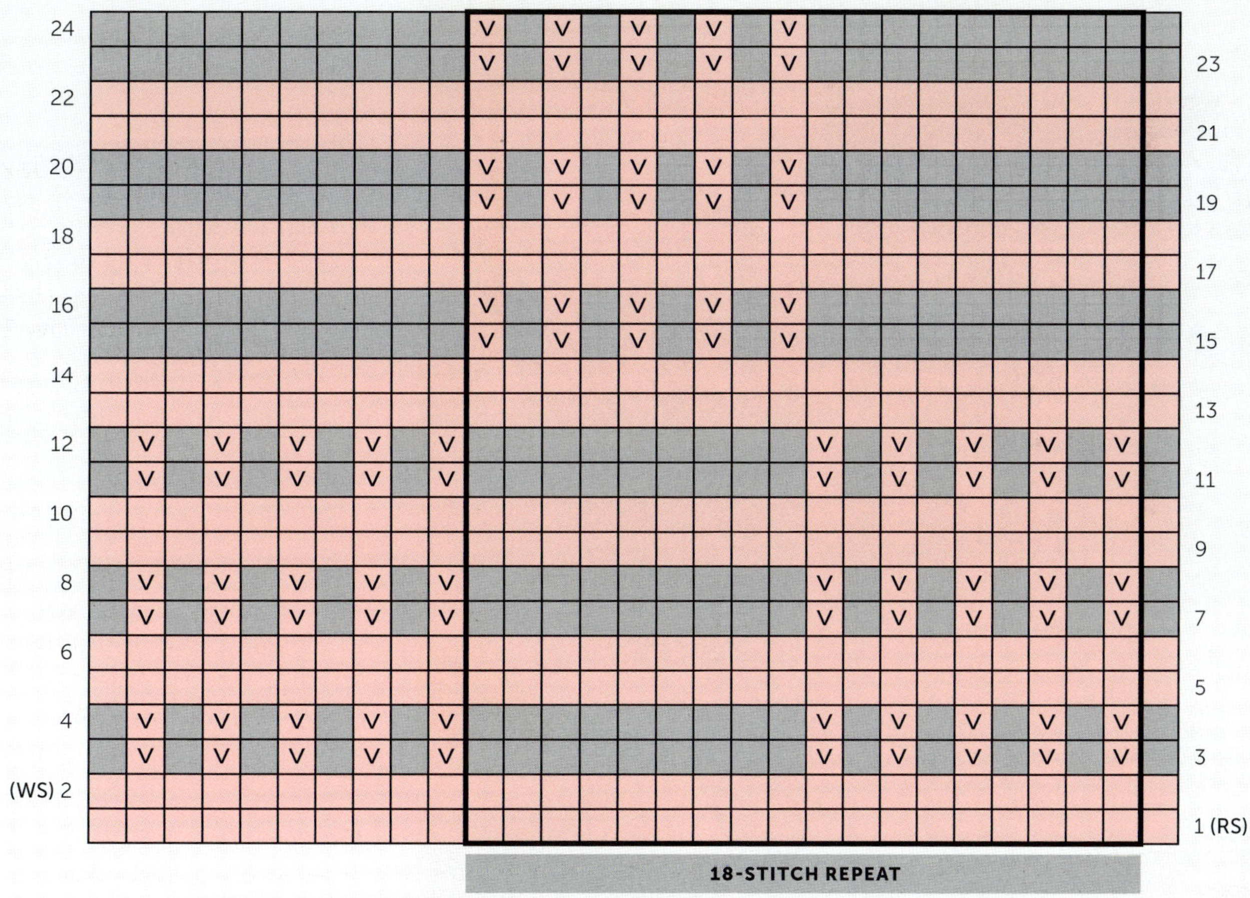

COLOR KEY

= A

= B

STITCH KEY

= Knit on RS; purl on WS

V = Slip the next st purlwise with the yarn to the WS

SAMPLER THROW

(combination stockinette and garter-based fabric)

EASY

Finished Measurement:
48" x 58"
(122 cm x 147.5 cm)

Gauge Information:
See individual Blocks for gauge.

Technique Used:
M1 ***(Figs. 6a & b, page 62)***

SHOPPING LIST

- **Yarn** (Medium Weight) 4 MEDIUM **[**3.5 ounces, 170 yards (100 grams, 156 meters) per skein**]**:
  - Color A (Grey) - 8 skeins
  - Color B (Linen) - 6 skeins
- **Knitting Needles**
  36" (91.5 cm) Circular,
  - Size 8 (5 mm) **and**
  - Size 9 (5.5 mm) **or** sizes needed for gauge
- **Additional Supplies**
  - Yarn needle

THROW

BLOCK #1 (Make 2)

Gauge: With larger size needle, in Jazzy Squares Pattern, 14 sts = 4" (10 cm)

With the larger size needle and Color B, cast on 47 sts.

Row 1 (Right side)**:** With Color A, knit across.

Row 2: With Color A, purl across.

Row 3: With Color B, K1, ★ slip 1 as if to **purl** WYB, (K1, slip 1 as if to **purl** WYB) 4 times, K9; repeat from ★ once **more**, (slip 1 as if to **purl** WYB, K1) 5 times.

Row 4: With Color B, (P1, slip 1 as if to **purl** WYF) 5 times, ★ P9, slip 1 as if to **purl** WYF, (P1, slip 1 as if to **purl** WYF) 4 times; repeat from ★ once **more**, P1.

Rows 5-12: Repeat Rows 1-4 twice.

NOTES:

Always slip stitches **purlwise** (page 6) with the yarn to the **wrong** side of the fabric.

When changing color, do **not** cut the yarn; instead, carry the yarn loosely up the side of the fabric.

The circular needle is used to accommodate the large number of stitches. Do **not** join at the end of the rows; instead, work back and forth in rows.

Row 13: With Color A, knit across.

Row 14: With Color A, purl across.

Row 15: With Color B, K1, ★ K9, slip 1 as if to **purl** WYB, (K1, slip 1 as if to **purl** WYB) 4 times; repeat from ★ once **more**, K 10.

Row 16: With Color B, P 10, ★ slip 1 as if to **purl** WYF, (P1, slip 1 as if to **purl** WYF) 4 times; repeat from ★ once **more**, P1.

Rows 17-24: Repeat Rows 13-16 twice.

Repeat Rows 1-24 for Jazzy Squares Pattern until piece measures approximately 27" (68.5 cm) from cast on edge, ending by working a **wrong** side row.

Bind off all sts in **knit**.

Jazzy Squares Pattern
(see CHART K below)
(multiple of 18 + 11 sts)

Use the Block #1 text, page 41, or follow the chart below.

CHART K: JAZZY SQUARES

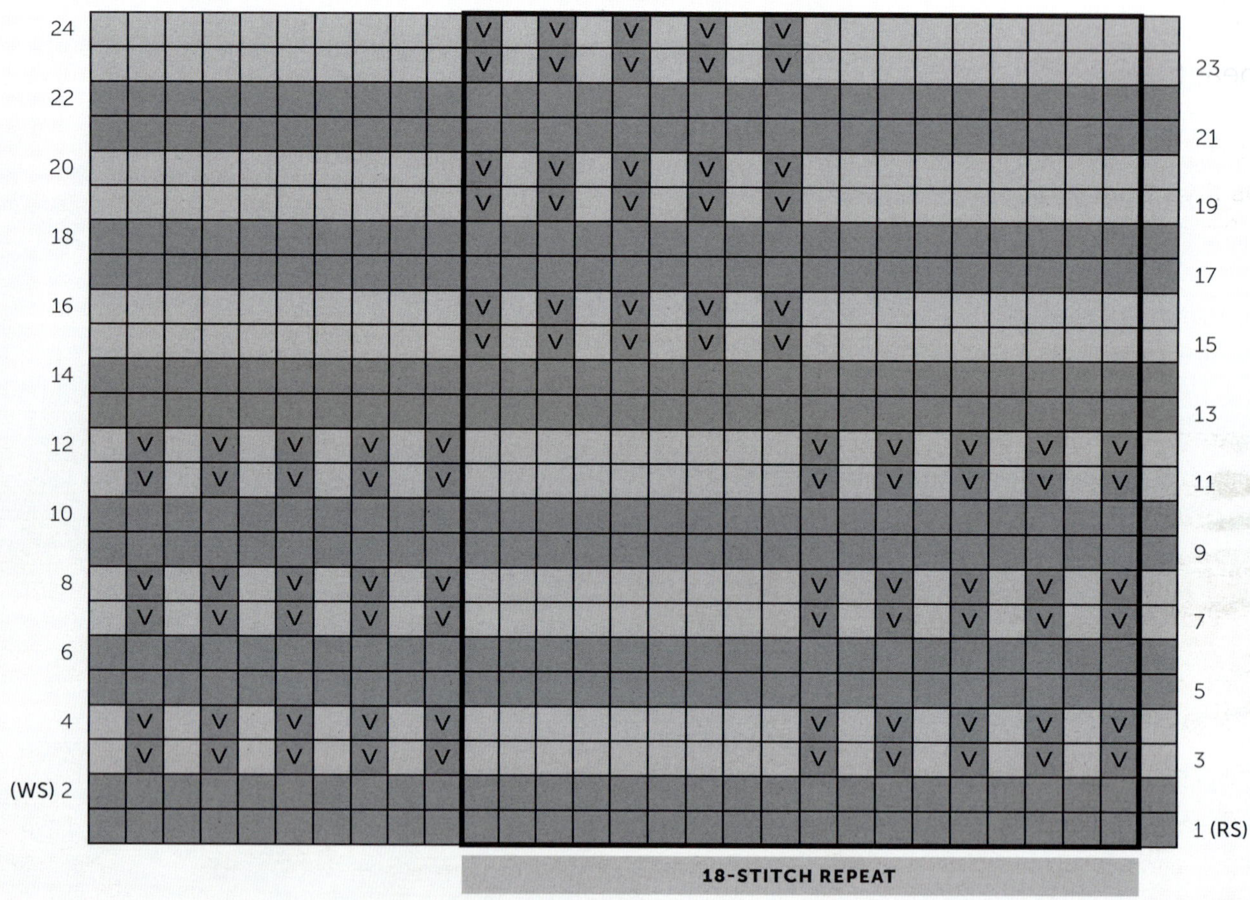

COLOR KEY

■ = A

■ = B

STITCH KEY

☐ = Knit on RS; purl on WS

V = Slip the next st purlwise with the yarn to the WS

BLOCK #2 (Make 1)

Gauge: With larger size needle, in Large Geometric Squares Pattern 16 sts = 4 (10 cm)

With larger size needle and Color B, cast on 97 sts.

Row 1 (Right side)**:** With Color B, knit across.

Row 2: With Color B, purl across.

Row 3: With Color A, K1, ★ K3, slip 1 as if to **purl** WYB, K4; repeat from ★ across.

Row 4: With Color A, ★ K4, slip 1 as if to **purl** WYF, K3; repeat from ★ across to last st, K1.

Row 5: With Color B, K1, ★ K2, slip 1 as if to **purl** WYB, K1, slip 1 as if to **purl** WYB, K3; repeat from ★ across.

Row 6: With Color B, ★ P3, slip 1 as if to **purl** WYF, P1, slip 1 as if to **purl** WYF, P2; repeat from ★ across to last st, P1.

Row 7: With Color A, K1, ★ K3, slip 1 as if to **purl** WYB; repeat from ★ across to last 4 sts, K4.

Row 8: With Color A, K4, slip 1 as if to **purl** WYF, K3, ★ slip 1 as if to **purl** WYF, K3; repeat from ★ across to last st, K1.

Row 9: With Color B, K1, ★ slip 1 as if to **purl** WYB, K5, slip 1 as if to **purl** WYB, K1; repeat from ★ across.

Row 10: With Color B, ★ P1, slip 1 as if to **purl** WYF, P5, slip 1 as if to **purl** WYF; repeat from ★ across to last st, P1.

Row 11: With Color A, K1, ★ K7, slip 1 as if to **purl** WYB; repeat from ★ across to last 8 sts, K8.

Row 12: With Color A, K8, ★ slip 1 as if to **purl** WYF, K7; repeat from ★ across to last st, K1.

Row 13: With Color B, knit across.

Row 14: With Color B, purl across.

Row 15: With Color A, K1, ★ K7, slip 1 as if to **purl** WYB; repeat from ★ across to last 8 sts, K8.

Row 16: With Color A, K8, ★ slip 1 as if to **purl** WYF, K7; repeat from ★ across to last st, K1.

Row 17: With Color B, K1, ★ slip 1 as if to **purl** WYB, K5, slip 1 as if to **purl** WYB, K1; repeat from ★ across.

Row 18: With Color B, ★ P1, slip 1 as if to **purl** WYF, P5, slip 1 as if to **purl** WYF; repeat from ★ across to last st, P1.

Row 19: With Color A, K1, ★ K3, slip 1 as if to **purl** WYB; repeat from ★ across to last 7 sts, K3, slip 1 as if to **purl** WYB, K4.

Row 20: With Color A, K4, slip 1 as if to **purl** WYF, K3, ★ slip 1 as if to **purl** WYF, K3; repeat from ★ across to last st, K1.

Row 21: With Color B, K1, ★ K2, slip 1 as if to **purl** WYB, K1, slip 1 as if to **purl** WYB, K3; repeat from ★ across.

Row 22: With Color B, ★ P3, slip 1 as if to **purl** WYF, P1, slip 1 as if to **purl** WYF, P2; repeat from ★ across to last st, P1.

Row 23: With Color A, K1, ★ K3, slip 1 as if to purl WYB, K4; repeat from ★ across.

Row 24: With Color A, ★ K4, slip 1 as if to **purl** WYF, K3; repeat from ★ across to last st, K1.

Repeat Rows 1-24 for Large Geometric Squares Pattern until piece measures approximately 19¼" (49 cm) from cast on edge, ending by working Row 2.

Bind off all sts in **knit**.

Large Geometric Squares Pattern
(see CHART L below)
(multiple of 8 + 9 sts)

Use the Block #2 text, page 43, or follow the chart below.

CHART L: LARGE GEOMETRIC SQUARES

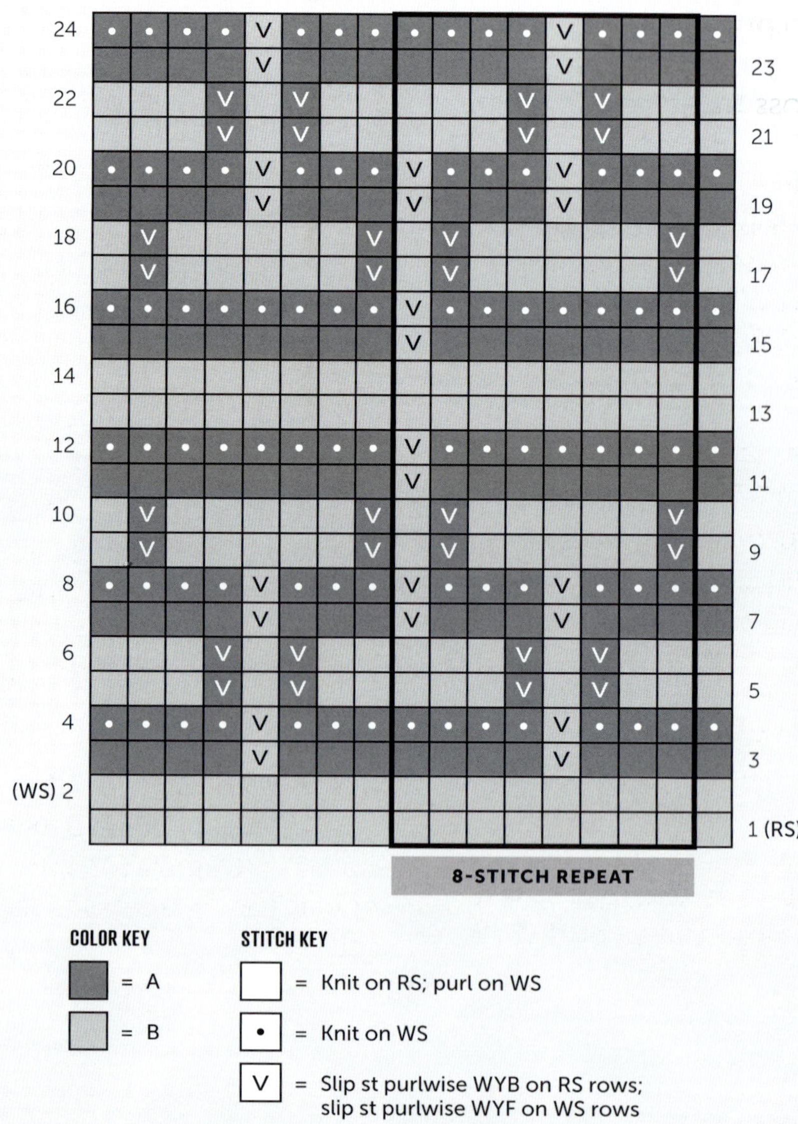

BLOCK #3 (Make 2)

Gauge: With larger size needle, in Turkish Tiles Pattern, 18 sts = 4"

With larger size needle and Color B, cast on 33 sts.

Row 1 (Right side)**:** With Color A, K1, ★ slip 1 as if to **purl** WYB, K9; repeat from ★ across to last 2 sts, slip 1 as if to **purl** WYB, K1.

Row 2: With Color A, K1, slip 1 as if to **purl** WYF, ★ K9, slip 1 as if to **purl** WYF; repeat from ★ across to last st, K1.

Row 3: With Color B, K1, ★ (K1, slip 1 as if to **purl** WYB) twice, K3, slip 1 as if to **purl** WYB, K1, slip 1 as if to **purl** WYB; repeat from ★ across to last 2 sts, K2.

Row 4: With Color B, K2, ★ slip 1 as if to **purl** WYF, K1, slip 1 as if to **purl** WYF, K3, (slip 1 as if to **purl** WYF, K1) twice; repeat from ★ across to last st, K1.

Row 5: With Color A, K1, ★ slip 1 as if to **purl** WYB, K3, slip 1 as if to **purl** WYB, K1, slip 1 as if to **purl** WYB, K3; repeat from ★ across to last 2 sts, slip 1 as if to **purl** WYB, K1.

Row 6: With Color A, K1, slip 1 as if to **purl** WYF, ★ K3, slip 1 as if to **purl** WYF, K1, slip 1 as if to **purl** WYF, K3, slip 1 as if to **purl** WYF; repeat from ★ across to last st, K1.

Row 7: With Color B, K1, ★ K1, slip 1 as if to **purl** WYB, (K3, slip 1 as if to **purl** WYB) twice; repeat from ★ across to last 2 sts, K2.

Row 8: With Color B, K2, ★ slip 1 as if to **purl** WYF, (K3, slip 1 as if to **purl** WYF) twice, K1; repeat from ★ across to last st, K1.

Row 9: With Color A, K1, ★ slip 1 as if to **purl** WYB, K1, slip 1 as if to **purl** WYB, K5, slip 1 as if to **purl** WYB, K1; repeat from ★ across to last 2 sts, slip 1 as if to **purl** WYB, K1.

Row 10: With Color A, K1, slip 1 as if to **purl** WYF, ★ K1, slip 1 as if to **purl** WYF, K5, slip 1 as if to **purl** WYF, K1, slip 1 as if to **purl** WYF; repeat from ★ across to last st, K1.

Row 11: With Color B, K1, ★ K1, slip 1 as if to **purl** WYB, (K3, slip 1 as if to **purl** WYB) twice; repeat from ★ across to last 2 sts, K2.

Row 12: With Color B, K2, ★ (slip 1 as if to **purl** WYF, K3) twice, slip 1 as if to **purl** WYF, K1; repeat from ★ across to last st, K1.

Row 13: With Color A, K1, ★ slip 1 as if to **purl** WYB, K3, slip 1 as if to **purl** WYB, K1, slip 1 as if to **purl** WYB, K3; repeat from ★ across to last 2 sts, slip 1 as if to **purl** WYB, K1.

Row 14: With Color A, K1, slip 1 as if to **purl** WYF, ★ K3, slip 1 as if to **purl** WYF, K1, slip 1 as if to **purl** WYF, K3, slip 1 as if to **purl** WYF; repeat from ★ across to last st, K1.

Row 15: With Color B, K1, ★ (K1, slip 1 as if to **purl** WYB) twice, K3, slip 1 as if to **purl** WYB, K1, slip 1 as if to **purl** WYB; repeat from ★ across to last 2 sts, K2.

Row 16: With Color B, K2, ★ slip 1 as if to **purl** WYF, K1, slip 1 as if to **purl** WYF, K3, (slip 1 as if to **purl** WYF, K1) twice; repeat from ★ across to last st, K1.

Row 17: With Color A, K1, ★ slip 1 as if to **purl** WYB, K9; repeat from ★ across to last 2 sts, slip 1 as if to **purl** WYB, K1.

Row 18: K1, slip 1 as if to **purl** WYF, ★ K9, slip 1 as if to **purl** WYF; repeat from ★ across to last st, K1.

Repeat Row 1-18 for Turkish Tiles Pattern until piece measures approximately 33" (84 cm) from cast on edge.

Bind off all sts in **knit**.

Turkish Tiles Pattern

(see CHART M at left)

(multiple of 10 + 3 sts)

Use the Block #3 text, page 45, or follow the chart at left.

CHART M: TURKISH TILES

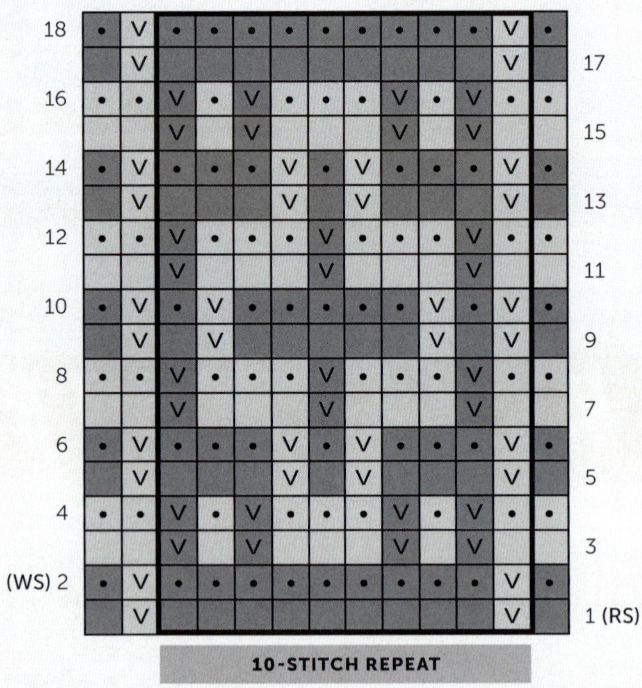

COLOR KEY

- Dark square = A
- Light square = B

STITCH KEY

- Empty square = Knit on RS; purl on WS
- • = Knit on WS
- V = Slip stitch purlwise with yarn to the WS

BLOCK #4 (Make 2)

Gauge: With larger size needle, in Ionic Tiles Pattern, 18 sts = 4" (10 cm)

With the larger needle and B, cast on 63 sts.

Row 1 (Right side)**:** With Color A, K1, ★ slip 1 as if to **purl** WYB, K5; repeat from ★ across to last 2 sts, slip 1 as if to **purl** WYF, K1.

Row 2: With Color A, P1, slip 1 as if to **purl** WYF, ★ P5, slip 1 as if to **purl** WYF; repeat from ★ across to last st, P1.

Row 3: With Color B, K1, ★ K1, slip 1 as if to **purl** WYB, K3, slip 1 as if to **purl** WYB; repeat from ★ across to last 2 sts, K2.

Row 4: With Color B, P2, ★ slip 1 as if to **purl** WYF, P3, slip 1 as if to **purl** WYF, P1; repeat from ★ across to last st, P1.

Row 5: With Color A, K1, ★ slip 1 as if to **purl** WYB, K1; repeat from ★ repeat from ★ across.

Row 6: With Color A, ★ P1, slip 1 as if to **purl** WYF; repeat from ★ across to last st, P1.

Row 7: With Color B, K1, ★ K1, slip 1 as if to **purl** WYB; repeat from ★ across to last 2 sts, K2.

Row 8: With Color B, P2, ★ slip 1 as if to **purl** WYF, P1; repeat from ★ across to last st, P1.

Row 9: With Color A, K1, ★ slip 1 as if to **purl** WYB, K3, slip 1 as if to **purl** WYB, (K1, slip 1 as if to **purl** WYB) twice, K3; repeat from ★ across to last 2 sts, slip 1 as if to **purl** WYB, K1.

Row 10: With Color A, P1, slip 1 as if to **purl** WYF, ★ P3, slip 1 as if to **purl** WYF, (P1, slip 1 as if to **purl** WYF) twice, P3, slip 1 as if to **purl** WYF; repeat from ★ across to last st, P1.

Row 11: With Color B, K1, ★ K5, slip 1 as if to **purl** WYB, K1, slip 1 as if to **purl** WYB, K4; repeat from ★ across to last 2 sts, K2.

Row 12: With Color B, P2, ★ P4, slip 1 as if to **purl** WYF, P1, slip 1 as if to **purl** WYF, P5; repeat from ★ across to last st, P1.

Rows 13 and 14: Repeat Rows 9 and 10.

Rows 15 and 16: Repeat Rows 7 and 8.

Rows 17 and 18: Repeat Rows 5 and 6.

Rows 19 and 20: Repeat Rows 3 and 4.

Rows 21 and 22: Repeat Rows 1 and 2.

Row 23: With Color B, knit across.

Row 24: With Color B, purl across.

Repeat Rows 1-24 for Ionic Tiles pattern until piece measures approximately 7¼" (18.5 cm) from cast on edge, ending by working a **wrong** side row.

Bind off all sts in **knit**.

Ionic Tiles Pattern
(see CHART N at left)
(multiple of 12 + 3 sts)

Use the Block #4 text, page 47, or follow the chart at left.

CHART N: ICONIC TILES

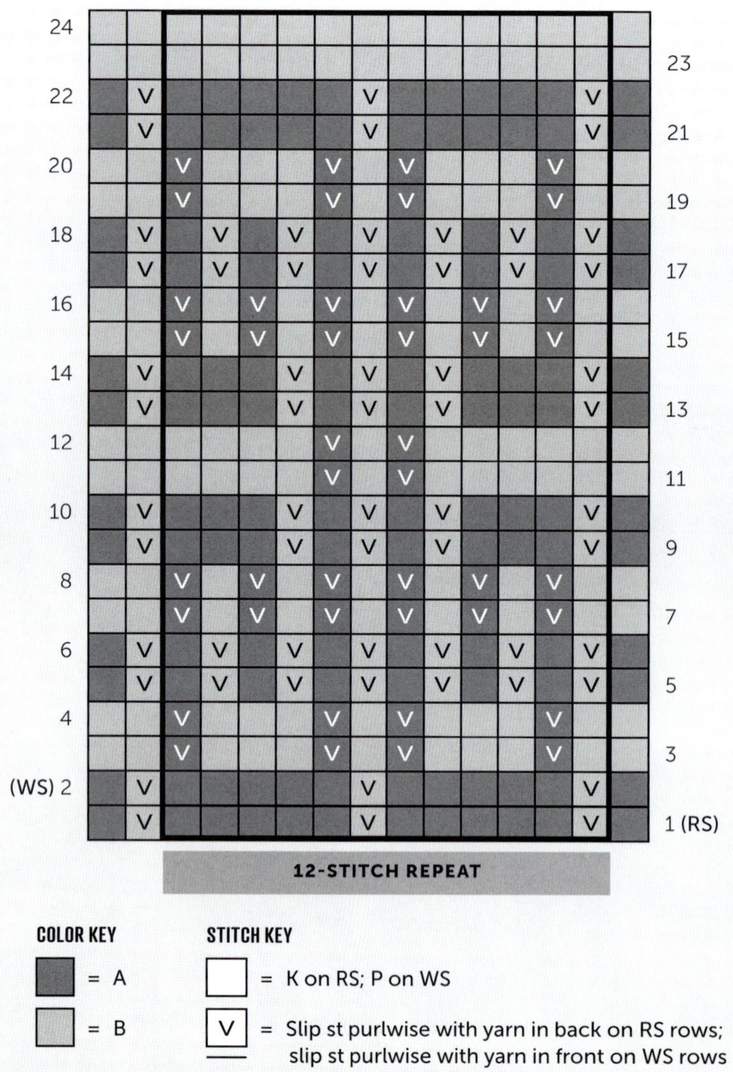

BLOCK #5 (Make 2)

Gauge: With larger size needle, in Small Geometric Pattern, 16 sts = 4" (10 cm)

With Color A, cast on 75 sts.

Rows 1 and 2: With Color A, knit across.

Row 3 (Right side)**:** With Color B, knit across.

Row 4: With Color B, purl across.

Row 5: With Color A, K1, ★ slip 1 as if to **purl** WYB, K3; repeat from ★ across to last 2 sts, skip 1 as if to **purl** WYB, K1.

Row 6: With Color A, K1, slip 1 as if to **purl** WYF, ★ K3, slip 1 as if to **purl** WYF; repeat from ★ across to last st, K1.

Row 7: With Color B, K1, ★ K1, slip 1 as if to **purl** WYB; repeat from ★ across to last 2 sts, K2.

Row 8: With Color B, P2, ★ slip 1 as if to **purl** WYF, P1; repeat from ★ across to last st, P1.

Row 9: With Color A, K1, ★ K2, slip 1 as if to **purl** WYB, K1; repeat from ★ across to last 2 sts, K2.

Row 10: With Color A, K2, ★ K1, slip 1 as if to **purl** WYF, K2; repeat from ★ across to last st, K1.

Row 11: With Color B, knit across.

Row 12: With Color B, purl across.

Repeat Rows 1-12 for Small Geometric Pattern until piece measures approximately 7¼" (18.5 cm) from cast on edge.

Bind off all sts.

Small Geometric Pattern
(see CHART O at left)
(multiple of 4 + 3 sts)

Use the Block #5 text or follow the chart at left.

CHART O: SMALL GEOMETRIC

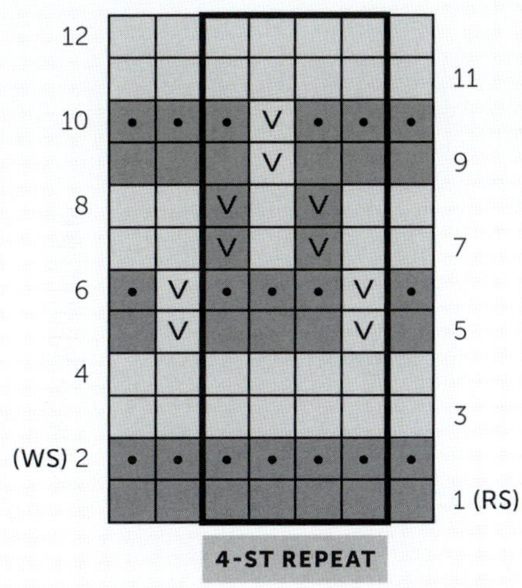

COLOR KEY

- (dark) = A
- (light) = B

STITCH KEY

- (blank) = Knit on RS; purl on WS
- • = Knit on WS
- V = Slip stitch purlwise with yarn to the WS

BLOCK #6 (Make 2)

Gauge: With larger size needle, in Trellis Pattern, 16 sts = 4" (10 cm)

With Color B, cast on 55 sts.

Row 1 (Right side)**:** With Color A, ★ K3, slip 1 as if to **purl** WYB; repeat from ★ across to last 3 sts, K3.

Row 2: With Color A, K3, ★ slip 1 as if to **purl** WYF, K3; repeat from ★ across.

Row 3: With Color B, ★ K1, slip 1 as if to **purl** WYB, K2; repeat from ★ across to last 3 sts, K1, slip 1 as if to **purl** WYB, K1.

Row 4: With Color B, K1, slip 1 as if to **purl** WYF, K1, ★ K2, slip 1 as if to **purl** WYF, K1; repeat from ★ across.

Repeat Rows 1-4 for Trellis Pattern until piece measures approximately 12¼" (31 cm) from cast on edge.

Bind off all sts in **knit**.

Trellis Pattern
(see CHART P below)
(multiple of 4 + 3 sts)

Use the Block #6 text or follow the chart below.

ASSEMBLY

With the **right** side facing, sew Blocks together following the Assembly Diagram *(see CHART Q at right).*

CHART P: TRELLIS

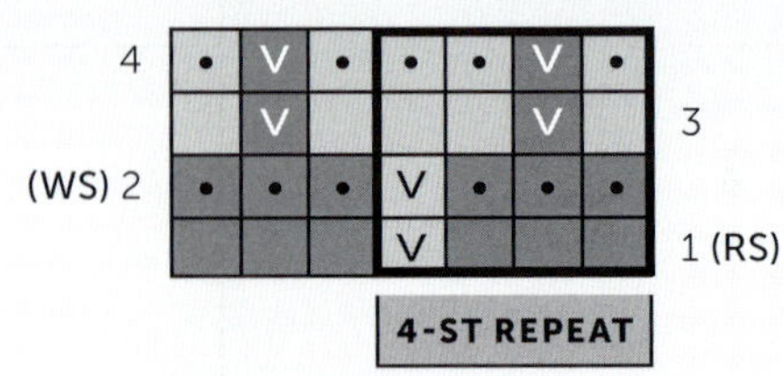

COLOR KEY

- (dark square) = A
- (light square) = B

STITCH KEY

- (blank square) = Knit on RS
- • = Knit on WS
- V = Slip st purlwiseWYB on RS rows; slip st purlwise WYF on WS rows

EDGING

SHORT SIDE

With **right** facing, using smaller size needle and Color B, pick up 174 sts evenly spaced across one short side of the Body ***(Figs. 7a & b, page 63)***.

Row 1 (Wrong side)**:** Knit across.

Row 2 (Increase row)**:** K1, M1, knit across to last st, M1, K1: 176 sts.

Rows 3-20: Repeat Rows 1 and 2, 9 times: 194 sts.

Bind off all sts in **knit**.

Repeat across opposite short side.

LONG SIDE

With **right** side facing and smaller size needle, pick up 202 sts along one long side of the Body.

Work same as for Short Side: 222 sts.

Repeat across other long side.

Sew each mitered corner.

CHART Q: **ASSEMBLY DIAGRAM**

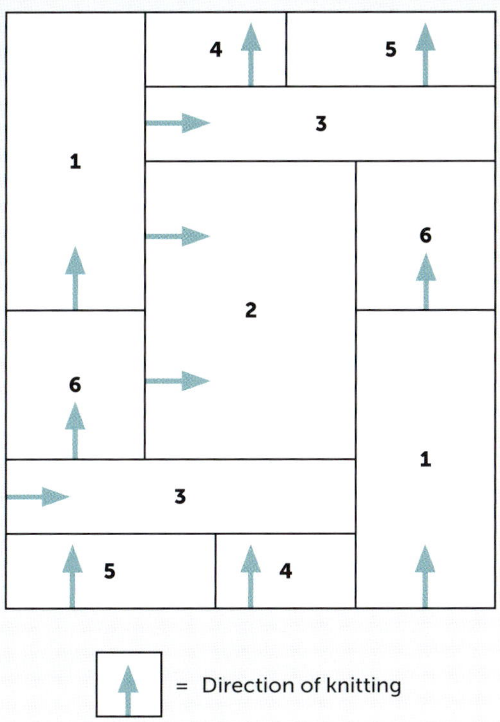

PULLOVER

(combination stockinette and garter-based fabric)

EASY

Finished Measurements:
Bust: {35½–39½}{43½-47½-51½}"/{90-100.5}{110.5-120.5-131} cm

Length: {24-24}{24½-24½-25}"/{61-61}{62-62-63.5} cm

Gauge Information:
With larger size needles, in Large Geometric Pattern, 16 sts and 28 rows = 4" (10 cm)

Techniques Used:
Decreases ***(pages 61 & 62)***
Increases ***(page 62)***

SHOPPING LIST

- **Yarn** (Medium Weight) 4 MEDIUM **[**3.5 ounces, 170 yards (100 grams, 156 meters) per skein**]**:
  - Color A (Periwinkle)-{3-3}{4-4-4} skeins
  - Color B (Aqua)-{4-4}{5-5-5} skeins
- **Knitting Needles**
  - Size 7 (4.5 mm) **and**
  - Size 9 (5.5 mm) **or** sizes needed for gauge
- **Additional Supplies**
  - Yarn needle

BACK

RIBBING

With smaller size needles and Color B, cast on {73-81}{89-97-105} sts.

Row 1: K1, (P1, K1) across.

Row 2 (Right side)**:** P1, (K1, P1) across.

Repeat Rows 1 and 2 for pattern until Ribbing measures approximately 2½" (6.5 cm) from cast on edge, ending by working Row 1.

BODY

Change to larger needles.

Row 1 (Right side)**:** With Color B, knit across.

Row 2: With Color B, purl across.

Row 3: With Color A, K1, ★ K3, slip 1 as if to **purl** WYB, K4; repeat from ★ across.

Row 4: With Color A, ★ K4, slip 1 as if to **purl** WYF, K3; repeat from ★ across to last st, K1.

Row 5: With Color B, K1, ★ K2, slip 1 as if to **purl** WYB, K1, slip 1 as if to **purl** WYB, K3; repeat from ★ across.

Row 6: With Color B, ★ P3, slip 1 as if to **purl** WYF, P1, slip 1 as if to **purl** WYF, P2; repeat from ★ across to last st, P1.

Row 7: With Color A, K1, ★ K3, slip 1 as if to **purl** WYB; repeat from ★ across to last 4 sts, K4.

Row 8: With Color A, K4, ★ slip 1 as if to **purl** WYF, K3; repeat from ★ across to last st, K1.

SIZE NOTE:

We have printed the instructions for the sizes in different colors to make it easier for you to find:

SMALL = **Aqua**

MEDIUM = **Pink**

LARGE = **Green**

1X = **Red**

2X = **Blue**

Instructions in **Black** apply to ALL sizes.

NOTES:

Always slip stitches **purlwise** (page 6) with the yarn to the **wrong** side of the fabric.

On **wrong** side rows worked with Color A, be sure to move the working yarn to the **front** before slipping stitches and then to the **back** to resume knitting.

When changing color, do **not** cut the yarn; instead, carry the yarn loosely up the side of the fabric.

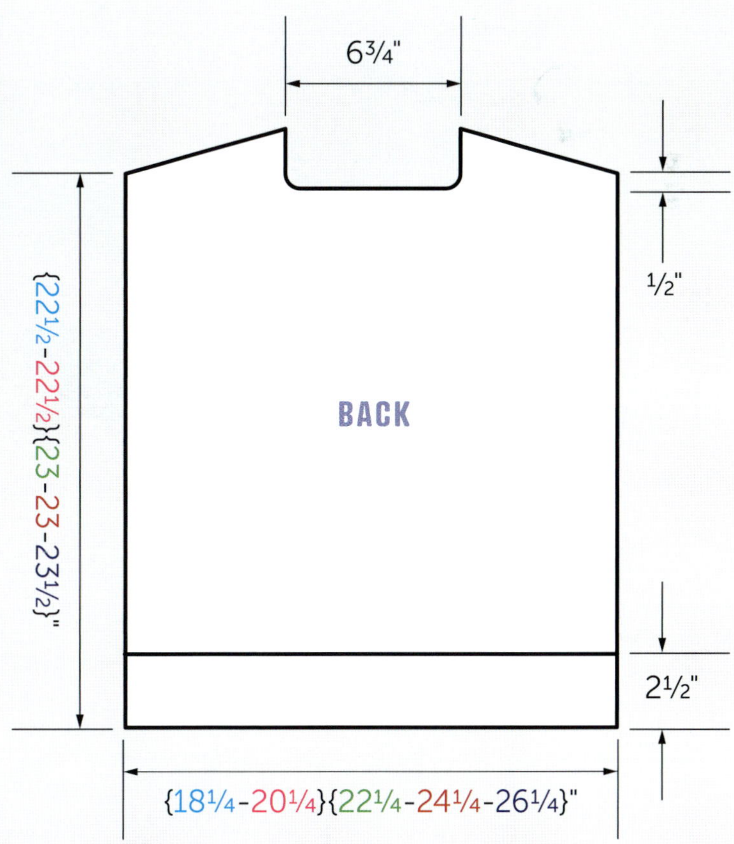

Row 9: With Color B, K1, ★ slip 1 as if to **purl** WYB, K5, slip 1 as if to purl WYB, K1; repeat from ★ across.

Row 10: With Color B, ★ P1, slip 1 as if to **purl** WYF, P5, slip 1 as if to purl WYF; repeat from ★ across to last st, P1.

Row 11: With Color A, K1, ★ K7, slip 1 as if to **purl** WYB; repeat from ★ across to last 8 sts, K8.

Row 12: With Color A, K8, ★ slip 1 as if to **purl** WYF, K7; repeat from ★ across to last st, K1.

Rows 13 and 14: Repeat Rows 1 and 2.

Rows 15 and 16: Repeat Rows 11 and 12.

Rows 17 and 18: Repeat Rows 9 and 10.

Rows 19 and 20: Repeat Rows 7 and 8.

Rows 21 and 22: Repeat Rows 5 and 6.

Rows 23 and 24: Repeat Rows 3 and 4.

Repeat Rows 1-24 for Large Geometric Pattern until piece measures approximately {22½-22½}{23-23-23½}"/{57-57}{58.5-58.5-59.5} cm from cast on edge, ending by working a **wrong** side row.

NECK SHAPING

Both sides of Neck are worked at the same time, using separate yarn for **each** side. Maintain established pattern throughout.

Row 1 (Right side)**:** Work across first {24-28}{32-36-40} sts, bind off the middle 25 sts, work across: {24-28}{32-36-40} sts **each** side.

Row 2: Work across to within 2 sts of Neck edge, decrease; with second yarn, decrease, work across: {23-27}{31-35-39} sts remain **each** side.

Work even until piece measures approximately {23-23}{23½-23½-24}"/{58.5-58.5}{59.5-59.5-61} cm from cast on edge, ending by working a **wrong** side row.

SHOULDER SHAPING

Rows 1-6: Bind off {6-7}{8-9-10} sts at the beginning of the next 6 rows, work across; with second yarn, work across: {5-6}{7-8-9} sts **each** side.

Row 7: Bind off all sts on first side; with second yarn, work across.

Bind off remaining sts.

Large Geometric Pattern
(see CHART R at right)
(multiple of 8 + 9 stitches)

Use the Body text, page 53, or follow the chart at right.

CHART R: LARGE GEOMETRIC

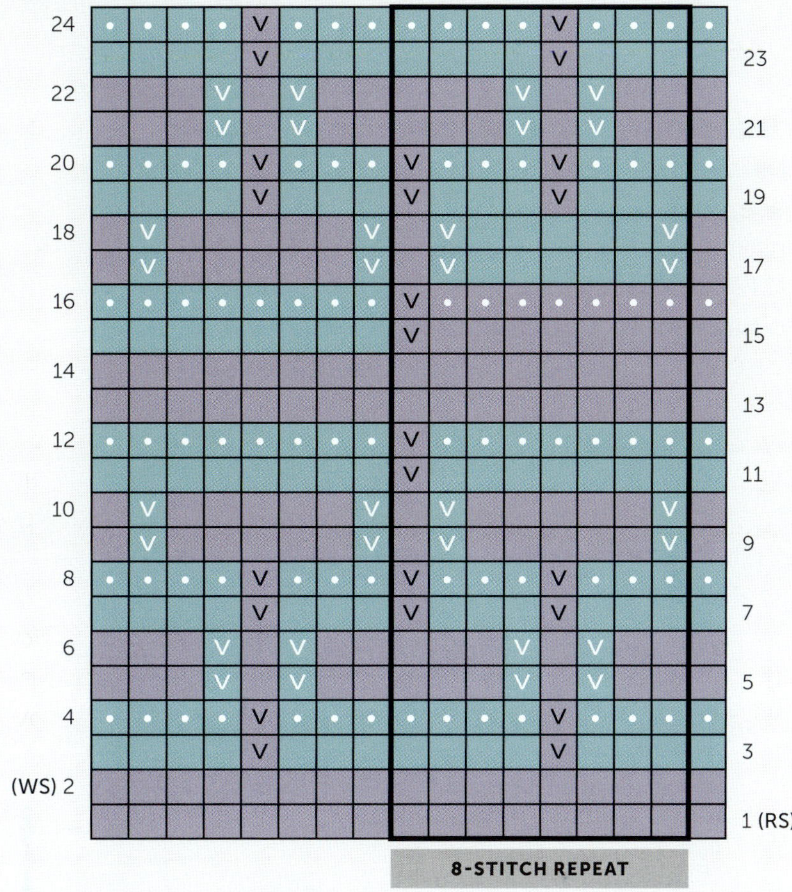

COLOR KEY

- ▒ = A
- ▒ = B

STITCH KEY

- □ = Knit on RS; purl on WS
- • = Knit on WS
- V = Slip st purlwise WYB on RS rows; slip st purlwise WYF on WS rows

FRONT

Work same as the Back until the piece measures approximately {21-21}{21½-21½-22}"/{53.5 53.5}{54.5-54.5-56} cm from cast on edge, ending by working a **wrong** side row.

NECK SHAPING

Both sides of Neck are worked at the same time, using separate yarn for **each** side. Maintain established pattern throughout.

Row 1 (Right side)**:** Work across first {30-34}{38-42-46} sts, bind off the middle 13 sts, work across: {30-34}{38-42-46} sts **each** side.

Rows 2 and 3: Work across; with second yarn, bind off 3 sts at Neck edge, work across: {27-31}{35-39-43} sts **each** side.

Rows 4 and 5: Work across; with second yarn, bind off 2 sts at Neck edge, work across: {25-29}{33-37-41} sts **each** side.

Rows 6 and 7: Work across to within 2 sts of Neck edge, decrease; with second yarn, decrease at Neck edge, work across: {23-27}{31-35-59} sts remain **each** side.

Work even until Front measures approximately {23-23}{23½-23½-24}"/{58.5-58.5}{59.5-59.5-61} cm from cast on edge, ending by working a **wrong** side row.

SHOULDER SHAPING

Work same as for Back.

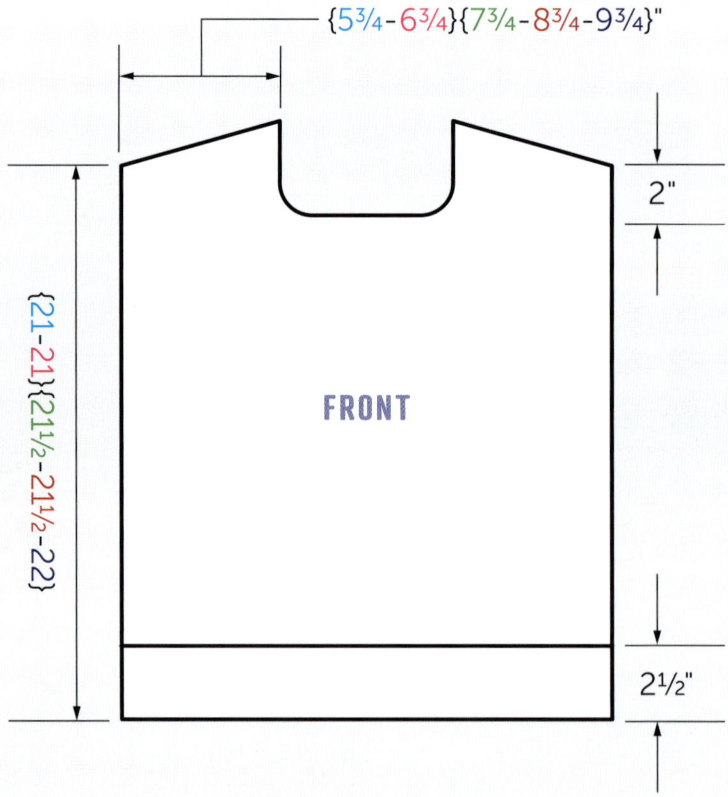

SLEEVE (MAKE 2)

RIBBING

With smaller needles and Color B, cast on 41 sts.

Row 1: K1, (P1, K1) across.

Row 2 (Right side)**:** P1, (K1, P1) across.

Repeat Rows 1 and 2 for pattern until Ribbing measures approximately 2½" (6.5 cm) from cast on edge, ending by working Row 1.

BODY

Change to the larger needles.

Work in Large Geometric Pattern and increase one st at each edge, every 4 rows, {0-0}{2-3-13} times; then every 6 rows, {6-8}{16-15-7} times; then every 8 rows, {10-8}{0-0-0} times while working the new sts into the pattern as they accumulate: {73-73}{77-77-81} sts.

Work even until the Sleeve measures approximately {19½-19}{18-17½-16½}"/{49.5-48.5}{45.5-44.5-42} cm from cast on edge, ending by working a **wrong** side row.

Bind off all sts in **knit**.

FINISHING

Sew one shoulder seam.

NECKBAND

With smaller size needles and Color B, pick up an even number of sts along Neck edge ***(Figs. 7a & b, page 63)***.

Work K1, P1 Rib for 1" (2.5 cm).

Bind off in the pattern.

Sew second shoulder seam including the side of the Neckband.

Place markers on Front and Back, {9-9}{9½-9½-10}"/{23 23}{24-24-25.5} cm down from shoulder seams.

Sew the Sleeves between the markers.

Weave underarm and side in one continuous seam ***(Fig. 8, page 63)***.

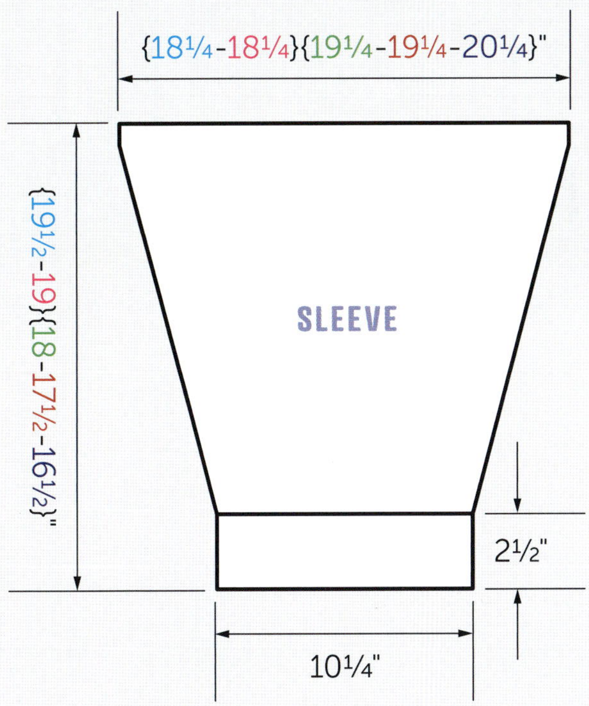

GENERAL INSTRUCTIONS

BBREVIATIONS

cm	centimeters
K	knit
M1	make one
mm	millimeters
P	purl
RS	right side
Rnd(s)	Round(s)
SSK	slip, slip, knit
st(s)	stitch(es)
tog	together
WS	wrong side
WYB	with yarn in back
WYF	With yarn in front

;YMBOLS & TERMS

★ — work instructions following ★ as many **more** times as indicated in addition to the first time.

) or **[ ]** — work enclosed instructions **as many** times as specified by the number immediately following **or** contains explanatory remarks.

:olon (:) — the number(s) given after a colon at the end of a row or round denotes the number of stitches you should have on that row or round.

vork even — work without increasing or decreasing in the established pattern.

;AUGE

:xact gauge is essential for proper ize and fit. Before beginning your roject, make a sample swatch in ne yarn and needles specified in ne individual instructions. After ompleting the swatch, measure it, ounting your stitches and rows/ ounds carefully. If your swatch is arger or smaller than specified, **nake another, changing needle ize to get the correct gauge**. Keep ying until you find the size needles nat will give you the specified gauge.

KNIT TERMINOLOGY

United States		International
gauge	=	tension
bind off	=	cast off
yarn over (YO)	=	yarn forward (yfwd) **or** yarn around needle (yrn)

KNITTING NEEDLES

United States	English U.K.	Metric (mm)
0	13	2
1	12	2.25
2	11	2.75
3	10	3.25
4	9	3.5
5	8	3.75
6	7	4
7	6	4.5
8	5	5
9	4	5.5

United States	English U.K.	Metric (mm)
10	3	6
10½	2	6.5
11	1	8
13	00	9
15	000	10
17	—	12.75
19	—	15
35	—	19
50	—	25

BASIC	Projects using basic stitches. May include basic increases and decreases.
EASY	Projects may include simple stitch patterns, color work, and/or shaping.
INTERMEDIATE	Projects may include involved stitch patterns, color work, and/or shaping.
COMPLEX	Projects may include complex stitch patterns, color work, and/or shaping using a variety of techniques and stitches simultaneously.

Yarn Weight Symbol & Names	LACE 0	SUPER FINE 1	FINE 2	LIGHT 3	MEDIUM 4	BULKY 5	SUPER BULKY 6	JUMBO 7
Type of Yarns in Category	Fingering, size 10 crochet thread	Sock, Fingering, Baby	Sport, Baby	DK, Light Worsted	Worsted, Afghan, Aran	Chunky, Craft, Rug	Super Bulky, Roving	Jumbo, Roving
Knit Gauge Ranges in Stockinette St to 4" (10 cm)	33-40 sts**	27-32 sts	23-26 sts	21-24 sts	16-20 sts	12-15 sts	7-11 sts	6 sts and fewer
Advised Needle Size Range	000 to 1	1 to 3	3 to 5	5 to 7	7 to 9	9 to11	11 to 17	17 and larger

* GUIDELINES ONLY: The chart above reflects the most commonly used gauges and needle sizes for specific yarn categories.

** Lace weight yarns are usually knitted on larger needles to create lacy openwork patterns. Accordingly, a gauge range is difficult to determine. Always follow the gauge stated in your pattern.

MARKERS

As a convenience to you, we have used markers to help distinguish the beginning of a pattern or a round. Place markers as instructed. You may use purchased markers or tie a length of contrasting color yarn around the needle. When you reach a marker on each round, slip it from the left needle to the right needle; remove it when no longer needed.

A split-ring marker is placed around the first stitch on the round to indicate the beginning of the round. Move it up at the end of each round.

KNITTING IN THE ROUND

USING CIRCULAR NEEDLES

When you knit a tube, as for a hat or cowl, you are going to work around the outside of the circle, with the **right** side of the knitting facing you.

Using a circular needle, cast on all stitches as instructed. Untwist and straighten the stitches on the needle to be sure that the cast on ridge lies on the inside of the needle and never rolls around the needle.

Hold the needle so that the ball of yarn is attached to the stitch closest to the **right** hand point. Place a marker to mark the beginning of the round.

To begin working in the round, knit the stitches on the left hand point ***(Fig. 1)***.

Continue working each round as instructed **without turning the work**; but for the first three rounds or so, check to be sure that the cast on edge has not twisted around the needle. If it has, it is impossible to untwist it. The only way to fix this is to rip it out and return to the cast on round.

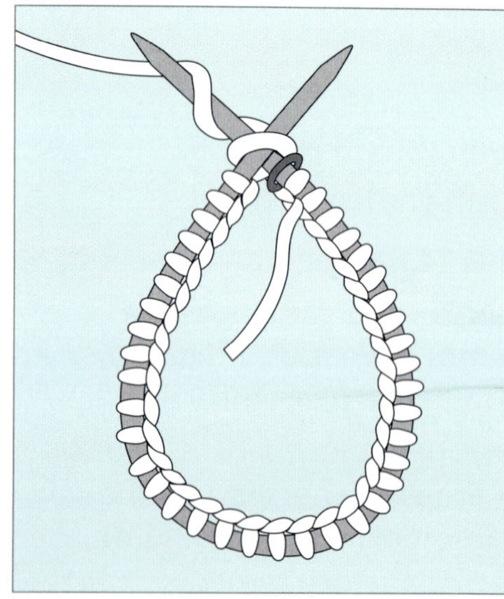

Fig. 1

USING DOUBLE-POINTED NEEDLES

When working a piece that is too small to use a circular needle, double-pointed needles are required. Divide the stitches between four double-pointed needles as specified in the individual instructions ***(Fig. 2a)***. Being careful **not** to twist the cast on ridge, form a square with the needles ***(Fig. 2b)***.

With the working yarn coming from the stitch on the last needle and using the remaining needle ***(Fig. 2c)***, work across the stitches on the first needle.

You will now have an empty needle with which to work the stitches from the next needle. Work the first stitch of each needle firmly to prevent gaps.

Continue working around without turning the work.

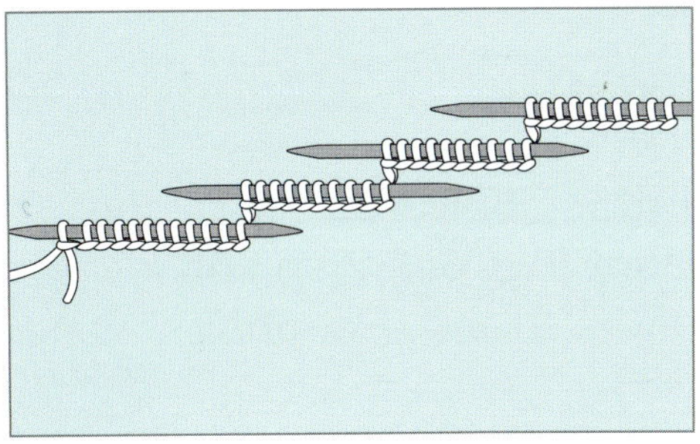

Fig. 2a

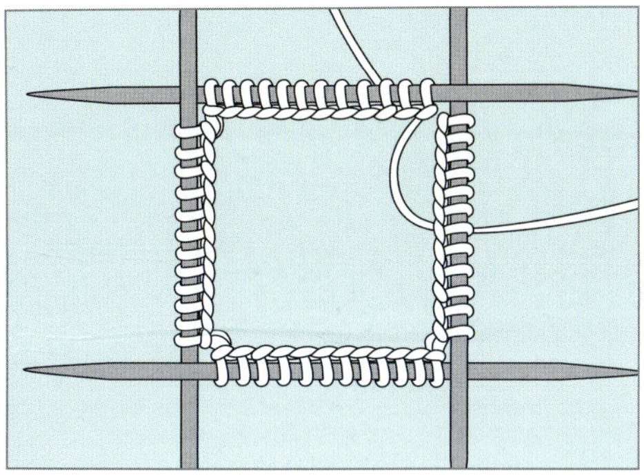

Fig. 2b

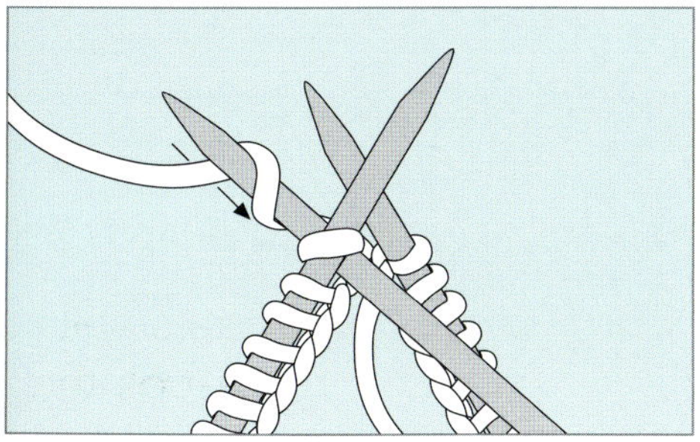

Fig. 2c

ZEROS

To consolidate the length of an involved pattern, zeros are sometimes used so that all sizes can be combined. For example, increase one st at each edge, every 4 rows, {0-0}{2-3-13} times means the first 2 sizes would do nothing, the third size would increase twice, the fourth size would increase 3 times, and the last size would increase 13 times.

DECREASES

KNIT 2 TOGETHER

(abbreviated K2 tog)
Insert the right needle into the **front** of the first two stitches on the left needle as if to **knit *(Fig. 3)***, then **knit** them together as if they were one stitch.

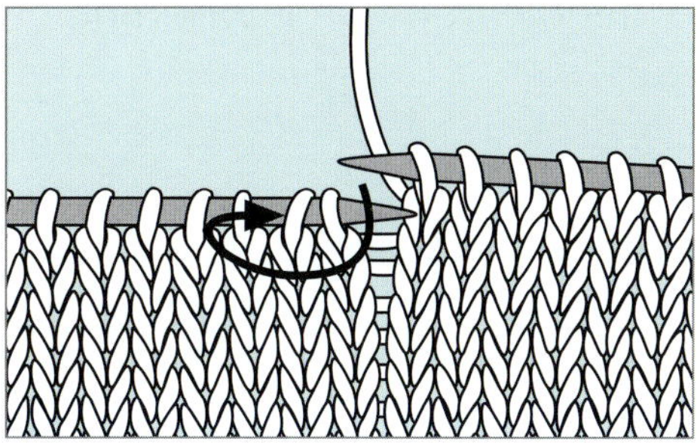

Fig. 3

PURL 2 TOGETHER

(abbreviated P2 tog)
Insert the right needle into the **front** of the first two stitches on the left needle as if to **purl *(Fig. 4)***, then **purl** them together is if they were one stitch.

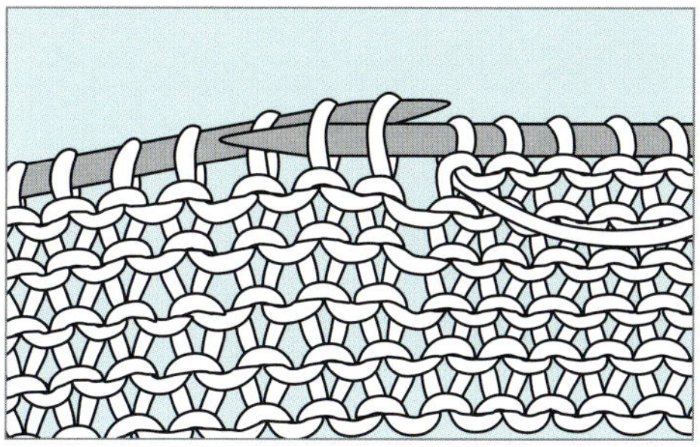

Fig. 4

SLIP, SLIP, KNIT

(abbreviated SSK)

Separately slip two stitches as if to **knit** ***(Fig. 5a)***. Insert the left needle into the **front** of both slipped stitches ***(Fig. 5b)*** and **knit** them together as if they were one stitch ***(Fig. 5c)***.

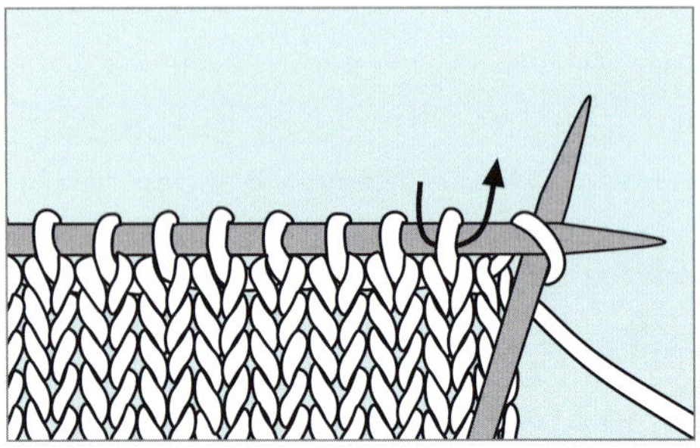

Fig. 5a

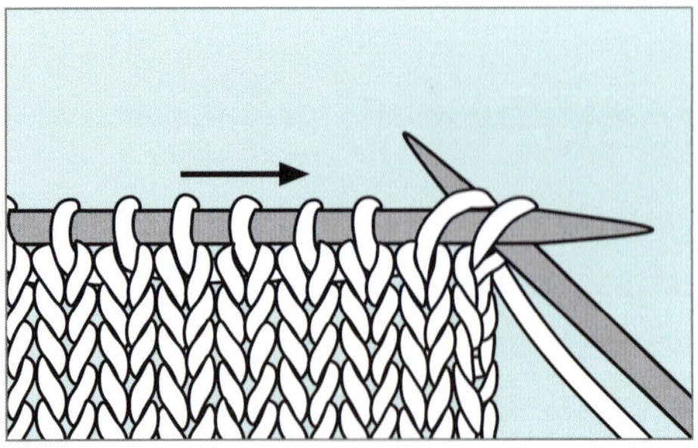

Fig. 5b

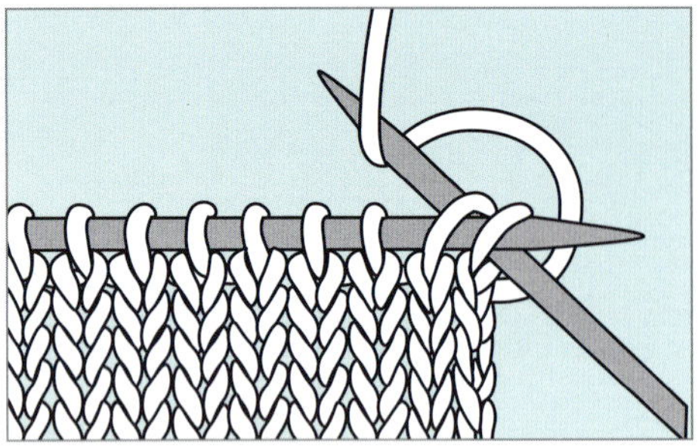

Fig. 5c

INCREASES

MAKE ONE

(abbreviated M1)

Insert the left needle under the horizontal strand between the stitches from the **front** ***(Fig. 6a)***, then **knit** into the back of the strand ***(Fig. 6b)***.

Fig. 6a

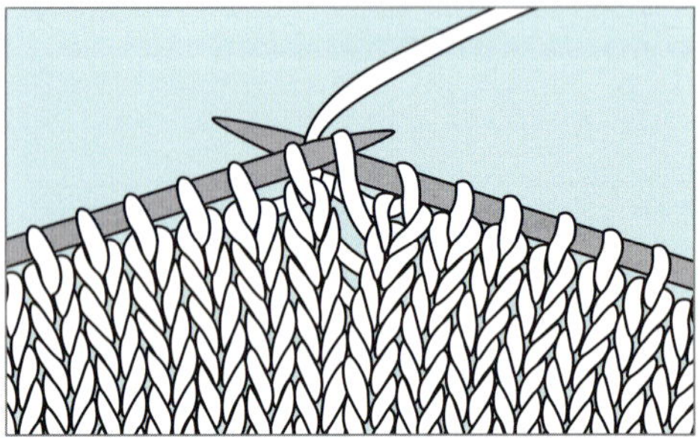

Fig. 6b

PICKING UP STITCHES

When instructed to pick up stitches, insert the needle from the **front** to the **back** under two strands at the edge of the piece ***(Figs. 7a & b)***. Put the yarn around the needle as if to **knit**, then bring the needle with the yarn back through the stitch to the right side, resulting in a stitch on the needle.

A crochet hook may be helpful to pull yarn through.

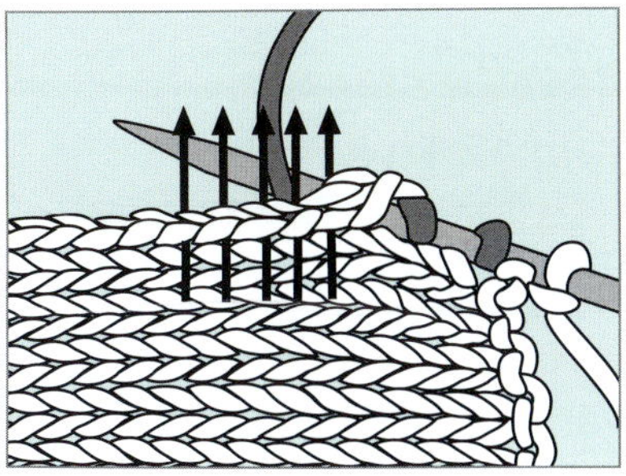

Fig. 7a

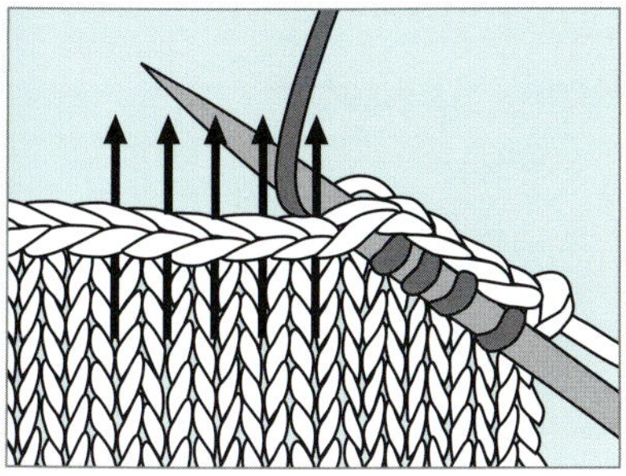

Fig. 7b

WEAVING SEAMS

With the **right** side of both pieces facing you and edges even, sew through both sides once to secure the seam. Insert the needle under the bar **between** the first and second stitches on the row and pull the yarn through ***(Fig. 8)***. Insert the needle under the next bar on the second side. Repeat from side to side, being careful to match rows. If the edges are different lengths, it may be necessary to insert the needle under two bars at one edge.

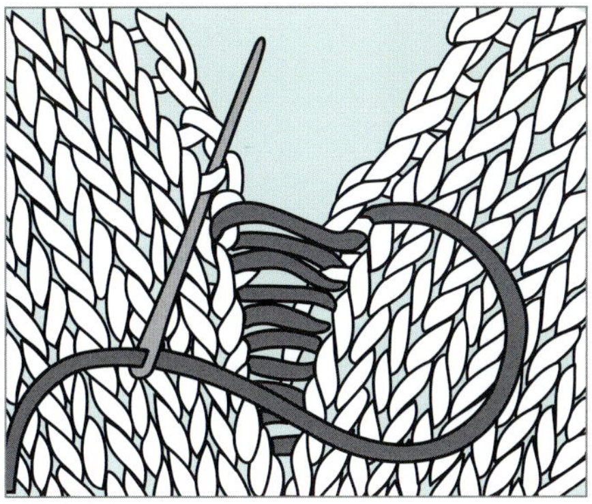

Fig. 8

Yarn Information

The projects in this book were made using Lion Brand® yarns. Any brand of yarn in the specified weight may be used. It is best to refer to the yardage/meters when determining how many skeins or balls to purchase. Remember, to arrive at the finished size, it is the GAUGE/TENSION that is important, not the brand of yarn.

For your convenience, listed below are the specific yarns and colors used to create our photography models. Because yarn manufacturers make frequent changes in their product lines, you may sometimes find it necessary to use a substitute yarn or to search for the discontinued product at alternate suppliers (locally or online).

HEADBAND

Heartland®

Color A—#172 Mesa Verde
Color B—#147 Hot Springs

HAT

Wool-Ease®

Color A—#102 Ranch Red
Color B—#099 Fisherman

COWL

Heartland®

Color A—#178 Pinnacles
Color B—#195 Biscayne
Color C—#156 Guadalupe Mountains
Color D—#098 Acadia

WRAP

Vanna's Choice®

Color A—#113 Scarlet
Color B—#158 Mustard
Color C—#169 Pistachio
Color D—#098 Fisherman

CRESENT SHAWL

Vanna's Style

Color A—#159 Mustard
Color B—#146 Fuchsia

BABY BLANKET

Vanna's Choice®

Color A—#101 Pink
Color B—#150 Pale Grey

SAMPLER THROW

Vanna's Choice®

Color A—#151 Charcoal Grey
Color B—#099 Linen

PULLOVER

Vanna's Choice®

Color A—#183 Periwinkle
Color B—#106 Aquamarine

We have made every effort to ensure that these instructions are accurate and complete. We cannot, however, be responsible for human error, typographical mistakes, or variations in individual work.

Projects made and instructions tested by Nancy Desmarais, Amanda Loggins, Rose May, Barbara Schou and Kay Shultz.

Production Team: Instructional/Technical Editor—Linda A. Daley; Senior Graphic Artist—Lora Puls; Graphic Artist—Michael Douglas; Photo Stylist—Lori Wenger; and Photographer—Jason Masters.

Copyright © 2019 by Leisure Arts, Inc., 104 Champs Blvd, STE 100, Maumelle, AR 72113-6738, www.leisurearts.com. All rights reserved. This publication is protected under federal copyright laws. Reproduction or distribution of this publication or any other Leisure Arts publication, including publications which are out of print, is prohibited unless specifically authorized. This includes, but is not limited to, any form of reproduction or distribution on or through the Internet, including posting, scanning, or e-mail transmission.

Library of Congress Control Number: 2019933476

Made in U.S.A